WORLD WAR II

THE ALLIED INVASION OF EUROPE

Peter Darman, Editor

ROSEN PUBLISHING
New York

This edition is published in 2013 by:

The Rosen Publishing Group, Inc.
29 East 21st Street, New York, NY 10010

For Brown Bear Books Ltd:
Editorial Director: Lindsey Lowe
Senior Editor: Tim Cooke
Military Editor: Peter Darman
Children's Publisher: Anne O'Daly
Art Director: Jeni Child
Picture Manager: Sophie Mortimer

Library of Congress Cataloging-in-Publication Data

The Allied invasion of Europe/[editor] Peter Darman.—First edition.
pages cm.—(World War II)
Includes bibliographical references and index.
ISBN 978-1-4488-9234-1 (library binding)
1. World War, 1939–1945—Campaigns—France—Normandy—Juvenile literature. I. Darman, Peter.
D756.5.N6A43 2013
940.54'21421—dc23

2012026314

Manufactured in the United States of America

CPSIA Compliance Information: Batch #W13YA: For further information, contact Rosen Publishing, New York, at 1-800-237-9932

Picture Credits:
Front Cover: Robert Hunt Library
All photographs: The Robert Hunt Library
All Artworks © Brown Bear Books Ltd.

CONTENTS

CHAPTER 1

PLANNING FOR D-DAY

The D-Day landings on June 6, 1944, remain the greatest amphibious assault of all time. The landings undoubtedly hastened the defeat of Nazi Germany, but they were also an enormous gamble by the Western Allies.

Previous pages: ***British soldiers practice getting over barbed wire defenses on a beach in southern England. By D-Day, the Allies were far more experienced at amphibious landings than they had been earlier in the war.***

In early June 1944, southern Britain was a vast armed camp. Huge naval, air, and land forces prepared for the most complex military operation ever attempted. The operation aimed to land large numbers of troops on the other side of the English Channel. The shore was heavily defended by the battle-hardened German Army.

D-Day was the product of a long period of decision making and planning. In December 1941, Hitler had declared war on the United States, shortly after the Japanese attack on Pearl Harbor. To some Americans, it seemed natural to concentrate on Japan, the country that had directly attacked the United States. Two weeks after Pearl Harbor, however, Britain and the United States met at the Arcadia Conference in Washington, D.C. They agreed that they would concentrate on defeating Germany before they turned to Japan.

The U.S. High Command worked out its strategy in 1942. The decision to defeat Germany first meant that the armies of the United States and Britain would have to invade northern Europe.

Britain drags its feet

What made this invasion more pressing was that in 1942 the Soviet Union was fighting a desperate campaign against Germany. Soviet leader Joseph Stalin appealed forcefully to President Roosevelt to engage major German land forces in northern Europe.

Britain's leaders, however, were reluctant to commit to an early invasion. There were many reasons for this. First, they argued that an amphibious landing was very risky. They pointed to the failure of the Dieppe raid of August 1942. This test landing on the French coast had been a disaster. The British believed that a huge force of landing craft would be needed for success.

U.S. troops march through the resort of Torquay before D-Day. The GIs faced resentment from some British troops, because they were better paid and supplied.

OPERATION BOLERO

The first U.S. service personnel arrived in Britain on January 26, 1942. They were a foretaste of what was to come. At the Arcadia Conference in December 1941, the Allied leaders decided to concentrate on the defeat of Germany before they combined to defeat Japan. The conference gave a high priority to the rapid buildup of U.S. forces in Britain, which were still small. The operation was code-named Bolero.

A few months later, the trickle of U.S. personnel across the Atlantic became more like a flood. By mid-January 1944, some 750,000 troops had sailed from Boston and New York. It took between five days and two weeks to make the crossing, during which time there was a danger of attack from U-boats. Over the next five months, an additional 750,000 men and their equipment arrived and moved into barracks in Britain. Bolero was the largest cross-oceanic troop movement ever.

THE RESISTANCE

Members of the Maquis and Free French troops study a map during the invasion of Normandy.

To support Operation Overlord, the Allies called on the help of about 100,000 members of the French Resistance. There were also some 40,000 members of the Maquis, groups of young Frenchmen who had gone into hiding to avoid being sent to Germany as forced labor.

Months before the landings, British and U.S. agents made their way into France, especially Normandy. They delivered arms and explosives to the Resistance, gathered intelligence, and carried out sabotage operations. Their main target was the rail system. Railroads were vital to the movement of German forces. In the event of an invasion, German troops would move by train to the point of attack.

The Resistance carried out raids on the railroads before, during, and after D-Day. Many railroad workers also staged permanent slowdowns and did not cooperate with the Germans. The Germans believed that it was this slowdown, rather than the Resistance or Allied bombings, that made France's rail system unworkable.

Dozens of RAF aircraft line up to take off at an airstrip in southern England before carrying airborne troops to France.

SPOTLIGHT

THE ATLANTIC WALL

Under the energetic direction of Erwin Rommel, the Germans reinforced the defenses of northern France in 1944.

Above: *This photograph, of Rommel (center) on another of his rounds of inspection, shows clearly the massive concrete defenses that the Germans had built along great stretches of the French Atlantic and Channel coasts.*

In April 1942, the Royal Navy rammed the gates to an important dry dock at the French port of St. Nazaire. In response, Hitler immediately ordered naval and submarine bases to be heavily defended. This was the beginning of what became Hitler's "Fortress Europe." By 1943 it was clear that Germany was on the defensive in the West, and so defenses gradually increased, becoming known as the Atlantic Wall.

The Todt Organization was tasked with building the wall's major fortifications. Thousands of forced laborers were used to create permanent fortifications along the Dutch, Belgian, and French coasts. Massive concrete structures were built.

In December 1943, Field Marshal Erwin Rommel was given the job of inspecting the defenses of the Atlantic Wall from Denmark to the Spanish border. He met the German commander-in-chief in the West, Field Marshal Gert von Rundstedt, that same month and they agreed that the most likely area for an invasion was the Pas de Calais in northern France—and that the defenses as they stood were unlikely to be able to hold out.

Rommel was placed in command of a newly created Army Group B that controlled the areas of northern France most likely to be attacked. He believed strongly that the Allies had to be stopped on the beaches, because once they had a foothold their control of the air would make it difficult for the Germans to bring up reserves.

Rommel set about improving the existing fortifications. Concrete pillboxes were built along the beaches; they contained machine guns, antitank guns, and light artillery. Mines and antitank obstacles were planted on the beaches themselves, and underwater obstacles and mines were placed in waters just off shore. Rommel himself drew sketches for how the obstacles should look and be emplaced, and almost six million mines were laid in northern France.

Further bunkers and minefields were placed inland, along key roads. To inhibit airborne landings, slanted poles with sharpened tops, which the troops called *Rommelspargel* ("Rommel's asparagus") were placed in likely landing areas, while some rivers and estuaries were flooded.

Right: *One of the large concrete emplacements built by the Todt Organization. These massive constructions were designed to be able to fire on landing craft and their accompanying naval vessels out at sea. The problem was that in order to protect against a landing over a 19-mile (30-km) stretch of coast, thousands of miles had to be fortified. This emplacement is in the Pas de Calais area. The actual invasion came further south, in Normandy.*

Left: *Field Marshal Erwin Rommel (foreground) on an inspection tour of the Atlantic Wall defenses. Rommel was determined to make it impossible for the Allies to gain a foothold on the coast of France.*

Below: *German troops marching into one of the great artillery strongpoints that were heavily protected to save them from the enormous weight of naval artillery and aircraft bombardment that they would face in any invasion attempt.*

Above: ***A battery proudly proclaiming that it was built by the Todt Organization. Fritz Todt was the Reich Minister for Munitions. He died in a plane crash in 1942, but his organization, which was a major exploiter of slave labor, carried on its work.***

Above: ***Iron girders cemented into the ground on the seafront of a French town to prevent tanks landing on the beach and moving inland.***

Below: ***Rommel and his staff inspect a beach at low tide covered with various types of beach obstacles. The wooden obstacles are pointing inland to snare landing craft moving off the beach to pick up additional troops and supplies.***

The British preferred a strategy of deploying forces in the Mediterranean. They claimed that attacks via the "soft underbelly" of the Axis—Italy—would be very effective. Finally, the British argued that Germany could be defeated by bombing its industrial centers.

Britain managed to delay planning for an invasion for many months. Eventually, however, Britain's leaders had to back down.

A strategy is agreed on

The countdown to D-Day began in January 1943. It started at the Anglo-U.S. Casablanca Conference in Morocco. The Allies made several key decisions. They agreed to establish a new body known as COSSAC (Chief of Staff to the Supreme Allied Commander). The Allies also decided that the transfer of U.S. troops and equipment to Britain—an operation code-named Bolero—would take place as soon as possible.

COSSAC's plans

COSSAC was led by Lieutenant-General Frederick Morgan. His British and American team had a number of responsibilities. It had to prepare a plan for an immediate invasion of Europe. It was unlikely that a chance would arise to carry it out, but the Allies wanted to be ready in case there was an unexpected event, such as the assassination of Hitler. It also had to devise a plan that would divert German forces away from the real landing. Finally, the team also had to mastermind Operation Overlord, the actual invasion plan.

The key question for COSSAC was where to launch the attack. The target had to be within range of fighter aircraft from southern England to provide air cover. After the initial landings, it was also important to land backup troops at least as quickly as German reinfor-

DWIGHT D. EISENHOWER

Some people thought that US General Dwight D. Eisenhower was an odd choice to command the greatest amphibious assault of all time. He had relatively little combat experience. Yet Eisenhower largely proved his doubters wrong. He had gained experience during the landings in North Africa in November 1942 and the subsequent capture of Tunisia in May 1943. He also put a lot of thought into his strategy. His decision to advance along a broad front in northwestern Europe in late 1944 is largely judged to have been correct. He also remained coolheaded when the Germans launched an offensive in the Ardennes in December 1944. The Allies soon took back the initiative from the Germans.

Eisenhower studies a map of France in his London headquarters in January 1944, when planning for D-Day was beginning.

cements could arrive. Morgan initially thought the best plan was to capture a port. He soon realized, however, that the Germans would plan to destroy any ports as soon as an invasion began.

Northern France

If Morgan could not capture a port, his second choice was a long stretch of wide, gently sloping beach. COSSAC thought that the French coast in Normandy was promising. It had good beaches that were not very well defended. They were also very close to the port of Cherbourg. However, using Normandy as a target would also present some problems. It was quite far from the vital fighter bases. It was also on a wide part of the English Channel, so the invading troops would have to endure a long sea crossing. If the Allies did not quickly capture Cherbourg, it might also be difficult to land supplies and reinforcements. COSSAC planned to build two small artificial harbors, known as Mulberries. PLUTO (Pipeline Under the Ocean) would carry fuel across the Channel from England.

The Allied High Command for D-Day. Front row (left to right): Air Chief Marshal Arthur Tedder, General Dwight D. Eisenhower, General Bernard Montgomery. Back row (left to right): General Omar Bradley, Admiral Bertram Ramsey, Air Chief Marshal Trafford Leigh-Mallory, Lieutenant-General W. Bedell Smith.

Landing craft move away from larger troop ships during a rehearsal for D-Day.

COSSAC's plan was approved by Allied leaders at the Quadrant Conference in Quebec in August 1943. In February 1944, COSSAC became part of SHAEF (Supreme Headquarters Allied Expeditionary Force), under the command of U.S. General Dwight D. Eisenhower. He and other senior commanders modified the plans. Instead of three beaches, they would land at five beaches across a 60-mile (96-km) front. U.S. forces would target two beaches, code-named Utah and Omaha. The British would land at two others, Gold and Sword. Juno Beach was allocated to Canadian forces.

SHAEF rejected trying to stage such a large landing at night. They also believed that the artillery bombardments that would start the landings would be more effective in daylight. The main assault force would land at low tide. The beaches would be at their largest, and the German underwater obstructions most exposed.

The next decision was to fix a date for the landings, code-named Operation Neptune. Because of the threat of storms in the Channel, no landing could take place before early summer. The night before the landings, airborne troops were to land to protect the flanks of the landing beaches. They had a better chance of success if there was a full moon. Taking these factors into account, the best conditions would occur on June 5, 6, and 7. The invasion date was set for June 5.

Keeping the plans secret

It was vital that the Germans did not discover either the landings' location or timing. The British stopped civilians traveling to the Irish Republic, where there were many German spies. They also created a 10-mile

(16-km) exclusion zone along parts of the English coast where forces were assembling. Only authorized personnel could travel within the zone. Diplomats from neutral countries were not allowed to enter or leave the country, in case they had gotten wind that something was happening.

False information also misled the Germans about the site of the landings. Fake radio signals convinced the Germans that the assault would take place at Pas de Calais, farther along the French coast from Normandy, in July.

German strategic debates

The Germans knew that an invasion would come, but disagreed about their best strategy. The Atlantic Wall, the name given to the defenses along Europe's western coast, was commanded by field marshals Erwin Rommel and Gerd von Rundstedt. They had different views on how to defeat any landings. Rommel believed that the invasion had to be stopped on the beaches. Von Rundstedt predicted that the Allies would be able to get ashore. He argued that a large mobile force should be kept in reserve to strike at the Allies once they were inland.

German preparations

Hitler still believed the main Allied landing would come near Pas de Calais. He kept most of his forces there. After he took up his command of Army Group B, Rommel began strengthening the Atlantic Wall. He built new obstacles to prevent vessels landing from the sea, and blocked the exits from the beaches. He built gun

These Duplex Drive Sherman tanks are being used in the crossing of the Rhine River in 1945.

THE FUNNIES

The British 79th Armored Division was a unit of specialized armored vehicles. They were designed to be able to cross a wide range of both man-made and natural obstacles. The unconventional tracked vehicles were nicknamed "Funnies." There were a number of variations. Most were based on modified British Churchill or U.S. Sherman tanks. They included the Sherman Crab, which had a rotating flail made of chains that could detonate mines or cut through barbed wire. The Centaur was a turretless tank fitted with bulldozer blades. The Ark was a turretless Churchill that had a hydraulic bridge. It lowered the bridge to cross antitank ditches and other wide gaps.

Other vehicles unraveled long strips of canvas from large bobbins. The canvas formed a roadway for other vehicles across soft sand. Another Funny fired trash-can-shaped shells to demolish concrete positions. One of the most useful was the Sherman Duplex Drive, which was an amphibious tank. The Funnies were among the first Allied forces to land on D-Day.

positions at key points. Rommel's efforts were disrupted, however, by Allied air raids. The French Resistance also carried out acts of sabotage.

From early April, Allied aircraft dropped some 200,000 tons (203,209 tonnes) of bombs on northern France. They bombed railroads and airfields, coastal defenses, radar stations, and military compounds. By D-Day the Allies had air superiority over the beaches. This would hamper German counterattacks.

Loaded landing craft speed toward the Normandy coast. In the background is the heavy cruiser USS Augusta.

Eisenhower gives the "Go" order

On May 29, Allied troops began moving to the ports along the south coast of England where they would board their ships. By June 3, everything was ready. The next day, however, the weather changed for the worse, with high winds and low clouds. That evening Eisenhower's weather expert, Group Captain James Stagg, offered some hope. Starting on the afternoon of the next day, June 5, there would be an improvement in the weather. It would last for about 24 hours. On the morning of June 5, Stagg confirmed his forecast. Within a few hours, some 7,000 warships and landing craft were heading for Normandy.

Allied vehicles already line the shore as U.S. infantry land on Omaha Beach late on June 6, 1944.

CHAPTER 2
D-DAY

In the early hours of June 6, 1944, thousands of Allied airborne troops were landed by parachute and glider behind German lines in Normandy, tasked with capturing key bridges and road junctions. Though the airborne landings were beset by problems, the German response was confused. Then Allied warships began pounding enemy positions onshore before landing craft began disgorging troops onto Utah, Omaha, Sword, Juno, and Gold beaches.

Previous pages: **U.S. assault troops huddle behind the protective front of a landing craft as it nears the beachhead at Omaha. Nerves would have been shredded at the sight of the carnage ahead.**

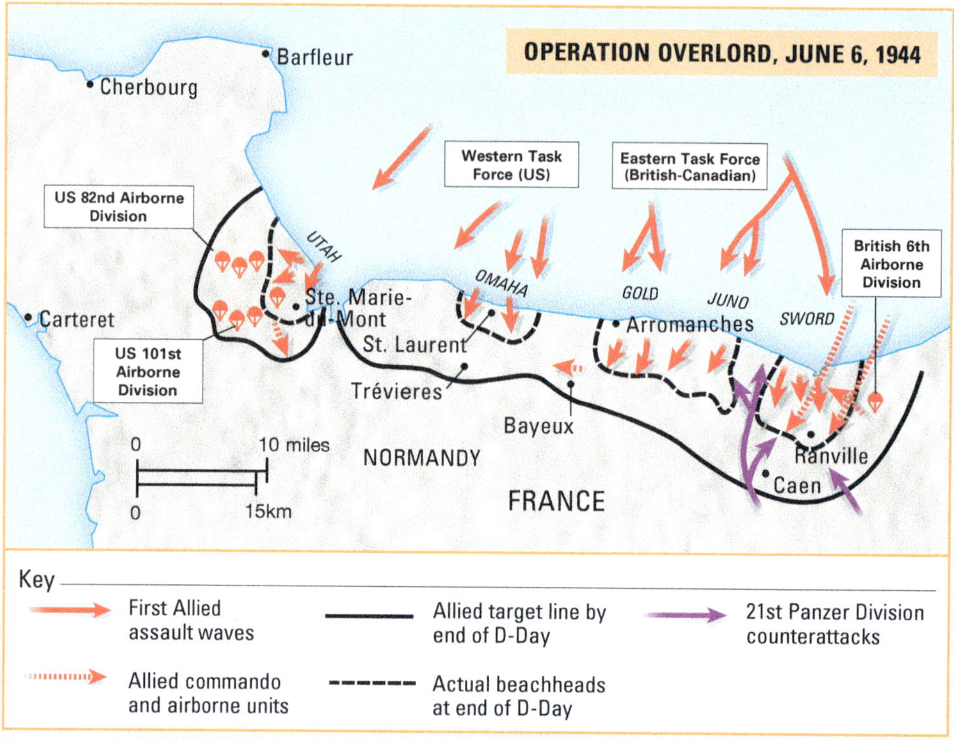

The five invasion beaches were all captured on D-Day. However, hopes of seizing an inland town or a port were not realized.

Men of the British 6th Airborne Division unload a jeep and other equipment from a glider on D-Day.

These U.S. paratroopers, on their way to France, were some of the first Allied troops in Normandy. About 23,500 paratroopers were dropped to protect the flanks of the invasion beaches.

Shortly after midnight on June 6, about 23,500 U.S. and British paratroopers landed along the edges of the invasion beaches. Their mission was to seize vital bridges and communications centers. They also had to hold off any German counterattacks until they were relieved by the amphibious forces. The airborne landings were largely successful. Some U.S. troops missed their target and ended up scattered over the countryside. The fact that they were so spread out confused the local German forces, who did not know what was happening.

The main amphibious landings took place after an artillery bombardment from some 200 Allied warships at about 0530 hours. German positions also came under attack from Allied medium and heavy bombers. They were part of the 11,500 aircraft committed to D-Day. They bombed the Germans on and behind the five landing beaches.

Success on Utah Beach

U.S. troops landed on Utah Beach at 0631 hours. They were just a minute behind schedule. Strong currents and inaccurate navigation meant that they were a little away from their precise target. They landed about 1 mile (1.6 km) south. The beach there was relatively undefended. The troops soon knocked out the only concrete gun position guarding the beach. Demolition teams cleared paths

Eyewitness Report:

"We were really just pinned down and couldn't really see anyone to shoot at. Around 10 o'clock things looked really hopeless on our part of the beach. They weren't bringing anyone else in because there was no use just piling them up on top of the ones that were already there. I saw a flat barge loaded solid with tanks. They were trying to get it in, and I guess the Navy must have known just how far those mortar shells could reach, because that raft was moving parallel to the beach, back and forth and just out of range. I did see a halftrack get in to the beach , and there were several that got hit, and one whole LCT (Landing Craft, Tank) loaded with halftracks caught fire and blew up. That was a Fourth of July fireworks."

***John Zmudzinski,* assault engineer, describes Omaha Beach, D-Day**

through the beach obstacles. By 0900 hours, the first tanks had crossed the Atlantic Wall. They fanned out into the countryside beyond to link up with the paratroopers. By nightfall on D-Day, some 23,000 men and 1,700 vehicles had gone ashore. The beach had been highly congested for much of the day. The cost of the assault had been 197 men killed and 60 presumed drowned.

The assault on Omaha Beach

Utah was a triumph. Ten miles (16 km) to the east, however, Omaha Beach was nearly a disaster. The U.S. troops were unable to get off the beach to make room for later waves of invaders. The fight for Omaha was the most difficult of D-Day. There were better defenses

U.S. troops help a wounded colleague after their landing craft was sunk off Omaha Beach. The Americans at Omaha suffered about 3,000 dead and injured.

Blood arrives at a Normandy airstrip ready for U.S. troops wounded in the campaign to break out from the beaches.

there than on the other beaches, and the German defenders were more battle-hardened. They were positioned on high ground, from which they could pour fire down on the attackers.

The Allies also made mistakes. The naval bombardment ended too soon, and the bombers missed their targets. Commanders launched landing craft and amphibious tanks too far out from the beach. Many were sunk. Many assault troops who reached the beach were seasick.

When the first amphibious assault wave landed on Omaha at 0630 hours, it faced a barrage of German fire. Within minutes, it was pinned down. By 0900 hours, some men were thinking of evacuation. However, inch by inch, small groups of troops began to make it off the beach to the high ground beyond. Others soon followed. By dusk, some 30,000 men were ashore, although most were still crowded on the beach. The high ground beyond was only thinly held by exhausted survivors of the first assault waves. Some 2,300 U.S. troops had been killed in the landings. The operation had come close to disaster.

English and Canadian landings

The three Anglo-Canadian beaches—Gold, Sword, and Juno—stretched for some 25 miles (40 km). They were wide and open, and ideal for amphibious landings. The coast beyond the beaches was flat.

German troops enter captivity on June 6, 1944.

SPOTLIGHT

THE AIRBORNE LANDINGS ON D-DAY

Airborne forces were critical to the success of Overlord. They had to secure the vulnerable flanks of the invasion area.

The British 6th Airborne Division and the U.S. 82nd and 101st Airborne Divisions were the first elements of the invading army to land in occupied Europe. Some were glider-borne and some landed by parachute. They had the task of stopping any immediate German response against the flanks of the main landing area, holding on until relieved by troops from the beaches.

In the east, the Allied High Command was most worried about the 21st Panzer Division, stationed near Caen, and so British glider-borne forces were dropped onto bridges over the Orne River and the Caen Canal. They overwhelmed the defenders in a matter of minutes. They were followed by additional units of the 6th Airborne, which had the task of capturing key coastal batteries and five bridges over the Dives River. Most of these tasks were accomplished by daybreak. Few of the transports strayed off course, and the German response was patchy.

In particular, the dangerously sited Merville Battery overlooking Sword Beach was taken by the 9th Parachute Battalion, and was therefore unable to fire on the invading forces. Four assault groups under Lieutenant-Colonel Terence Otway took the heavily defended emplacement by 0500 hours on June 6, improvising a new plan of attack after problems with bombing support and glider reinforcements.

At the far western end of the invasion beaches, the U.S. airborne divisions were tasked with capturing bridges and causeways across the low-lying, partly flooded areas behind Utah Beach. The first landings were due to take place at 0130 hours on June 6, but things went wrong from the start. Low clouds and enemy fire led to some transports dropping the troops in the wrong place, and some 75 percent of the paratroops landed outside their allocated drop zones. Many drowned in the marshy terrain, while others formed small groups that attacked German positions. Only one of the major objectives, the village of Ste-Mere-Eglise, was secured by dawn.

However, although the U.S. airborne forces had not done what was hoped, their scattered, haphazard landings confused the German defenders around the mouth of the Vire River, and so contributed to the fact that the Utah Beach landings went smoothly.

Above: U.S. paratroopers prepare to board a C-46 Curtis Commando aircraft during a training exercise for D-Day in southern England. Parachute drops were vulnerable to weather conditions, especially wind or cloud cover.

Left: U.S. paratroopers communicate with a member of the French Resistance about the location of German positions. They are some of the lucky ones who did not perish during the initial scattered parachute drops.

Above: *A C-47 Dakota prepares for takeoff. The C-47 was the most versatile transport employed by the Allies. For carrying and launching paratroops a special variant, the C-53 Skytrooper, was developed.*

Left: *Two British 6th Airborne lance-corporals guard a crossroads near Ranville in Normandy on June 6. The glider in which they landed can be seen in the background. They are armed with the standard British Army submachine gun, the Sten gun.*

Below: *U.S. paratroopers board their C-47 with the bulky equipment they had to carry onto the aircraft.*

The first waves came ashore at around 0730 hours. The British on Gold and Sword quickly crashed though the Atlantic Wall. Their success was due partly to a range of specially developed armored vehicles known as Funnies. The Canadians at Juno had a tougher time. They faced rough seas and alert defenders. By late morning, however, they were also pushing inland.

How successful was D-Day?

Despite the horrors of Omaha Beach, overall Allied losses were far lower than expected. Some 6,000 U.S. personnel were killed, wounded, or missing, along with 4,300 British and Canadian troops. German losses totaled between 4,000 and 8,000. By the day's end, some 128,000 Allied soldiers were ashore. Many more were on their way.

Despite this success, however, the invaders had failed in one goal for June 6. They had not pushed inland as far as they had hoped. They still had relatively little room to maneuver or to accommodate the reinforcements who were rapidly arriving. Worst of all, they had not captured any of the major towns immediately to the south.

Towns such as Bayeux and Caen were the focal points of Normandy's east–west transportation arteries. The Allies hoped that Caen would provide a major base for further advances. British troops had moved to within 2 miles (3.2 km) of the town, but their advance had been stopped by German defenders.

Those 2 miles (3.2 km) would have great consequences. Caen went on to become the focus of the German response to the landings. The Germans fought back with great determination. They forced the Allies into weeks of bloody combat in which casualty rates soared.

CHAPTER 3

THE BATTLE FOR NORMANDY

The German reaction to D-Day was far from decisive. Many key commanders, including Rommel, were away from their headquarters on June 6. Counterattacks by the troops in Normandy were half-hearted, and Adolf Hitler delayed releasing the panzer reserves because of continuing fears of another possible Allied landing in the Pas de Calais.

Previous pages: ***U.S. troops come ashore at Normandy following the initial assaults. In the weeks after D-Day, troops, armor and supplies poured into the beachhead.***

It was not until June 7 that the first significant counterattack got under way, when the Waffen-SS *Hitlerjugend* Division slammed into the Canadians north of Caen.

British and Canadian troops came ashore on the eastern flank of the Allied invasion. Their objective was to swiftly capture Caen and then push armored divisions inland to complete the German rout. Rommel had other ideas.

For the next six weeks, Montgomery launched the British and Canadian troops forward in a series of set-piece battles of growing intensity, as more forces poured into the bridgehead and became available for action. First he sent forward the 7th Armored Division—the famous Desert Rats—on a daring outflanking attack to the west of Caen. German Tiger tanks ambushed the force and sent it reeling back to the bridgehead. Next, the British XXX and VIII Corps began Operation Epsom to envelop Caen, but four Waffen-SS panzer divisions concentrated to hammer them hard. Into July, Montgomery continued to chip away at the Germans until his infantry were at the gates of Caen.

To the west, the Germans were giving the Americans under Bradley a hard time in the difficult *bocage* country. Rommel was desperate to prevent the Allies capturing the port of Cherbourg, which would considerably ease their logistical problems. The defense was led by veteran German parachute and Waffen-SS divisions, but there were nowhere near as many German tanks facing the Americans as the British.

Solid alliance

During the first two months of the Battle for Normandy, all the Allied ground forces were under the command of Montgomery and his Twenty-First Army Group headquarters. Eisenhower was still back in England and had limited control over the unfolding battle. Monty's conduct of the early phases of the Normandy campaign is still very controversial, as rival Allied generals and their supporters pushed to demonstrate their contribution to the eventual victory. At the heart of Allied strategy was the need to ensure the British and American alliance remained solid. This was Eisenhower's area of expertise, but some of his subordinates lacked

British and American troops aboard landing craft stream toward the Normandy coastline on D-Day.

his skill at soothing egos and forging cooperation.

By the end of June the Germans had massed some 10 panzer divisions in Normandy, with more than 1,500 tanks and armored vehicles. Even though the British and Americans had more than double this number of tanks, an Allied breakthrough seemed elusive. The Soviets had also just begun a major offensive on the Eastern Front, which ripped the heart out of the German defenses and cost the Wehrmacht an additional 500,000 casualties. If the German line in Normandy could be breached, Hitler's Reich would never recover. The Allies had to strike soon.

To break this impasse, Montgomery proposed a new strategy. Rather than attempt a breakthrough along a broad front, the aim would now be for the British and Canadians to continue to pin the bulk of the German armor in the east around Caen to allow the

U.S. troops killed during the initial D-Day assault lie covered on the beach.

A German soldier lies dead outside the pillbox he was manning, overlooking the U.S. landing zone at Utah Beach.

Americans to break through on a narrow front in the west. Once through the German defenses, U.S. tanks would swing both west and east to capture the vital Brittany ports and ultimately to defeat the German forces facing the British and Canadians around Caen. Bradley liked the new plan, but fierce German resistance during the drive on Cherbourg meant that it took him longer than expected to develop his strategy and build up his forces, and thus as July wore on U.S. casualties rose. And as the Americans tried to batter through the *bocage*, there were some complaints that Montgomery was making GIs pay in blood for his pursuit of glory.

Patton was equally critical of Bradley's slowness to break through, commenting: "Sometimes I get desperate over the future. Brad and [Courtney] Hodges [commander designate of First Army] are such nothings. Their virtue is that they get along by doing nothing. I could break through in three days if I commanded. They try and push all along the front and have power nowhere. All that is necessary now is to take more chances by leading them with armored divisions and covering their advances with air bursts. Such an attack would have to be made on a narrow sector, whereas at present we are trying to attack all along the line."

Operation Goodwood

Bernard Montgomery then launched Operation Goodwood on July 18 in an attempt to outflank Caen from the east. Three British armored divisions, with almost 900 tanks, backed up by 10,000 infantry, 700 guns, and 2,000 heavy bombers, were to smash through the weakened German lines and break into open country.

The Germans weathered the massive bombardment, and an improvised line of

SPOTLIGHT

THE JULY BOMB PLOT

Dissident German officers almost succeeded in killing Hitler on July 20, 1944.

Within the German Army there had always been senior officers who distrusted Hitler and believed that it was their duty to remove him from power. However, the Nazi leader's popularity meant that they found it difficult to formulate an effective plan. They were also hampered by the fact that the Allies were demanding the unconditional surrender of Germany, and offered no opportunity to negotiate with a regime that managed to take Hitler's place.

By 1944, however, a small group of officers believed they had no choice. They were led by Claus Schenk von Stauffenberg, who had been badly wounded in North Africa and had a staff position that brought him into regular contact with Hitler.

The plot was code-named Operation Valkyrie. On July 20, at a meeting at Hitler's East Prussian headquarters in Rastenburg, Stauffenberg placed a briefcase holding about 2.2 pounds (1 kg) of high explosives under the table. He left the room on the pretext of making a phone call and the bomb then detonated.

Stauffenberg then left for Berlin, to carry out the next stage of the plot—to seize power in the capital and neutralize the SS and the Gestapo.

However, the plot failed. The bomb had not killed Hitler. Most of the force was absorbed by the heavy table and just three of his staff died. When Stauffenberg arrived in Berlin, the other conspirators had not been able to take the reins of power. Hitler's supporters in Berlin refused to cave in. Stauffenberg was arrested and shot that same evening.

The aftermath of the plot was brutal. Anyone remotely connected with the plot was arrested, and two active field marshals, Rommel and von Kluge, committed suicide.

Left: ***"I want them to be strung up like butchered cattle," was how Hitler described to Freisler how he wanted the conspirators dealt with. The convicted men were strangled with piano wire and then hung from meat hooks.***

Below: ***Not all of the conspirators were army officers. Here, Johannes Popitz, Prussian Minister of Finance (second from right) and one of the conspirators, is being sentenced to death. In all, 5,000 people were killed in Hitler's revenge for the attack.***

Left: *Hitler and Göring together at Rastenburg after the explosion. The fact that the hut in which the explosion took place had thin walls meant that much of the force of the blast went outward—a concrete bunker would have contained the blast and probably killed Hitler. On the far left of the photo is Wilhelm Keitel, commander-in-chief of the army. A staunch Hitlerite, he was not part of the plot.*

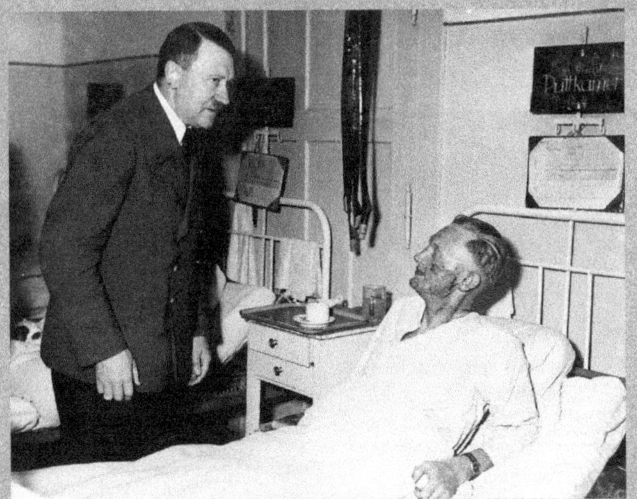

Right: *Hitler visits Admiral Puttkamer, who was badly wounded by the explosion. Three members of Hitler's staff died. Hitler had a special wound medal struck for those who survived the bomb blast of July 20. It was awarded to 24 recipients.*

Below right: *Erwin von Witzleben, a bomb plot conspirator and a retired field marshal, while on trial. He was not allowed a belt or suspenders and so in the courtroom struggled to hold up his trousers, for which he was berated by the court president, Freisler.*

Left: *Roland Freisler, President of the People's Court that tried those implicated in the plot. An ardent Hitler supporter, he screamed at the accused and tried to humiliate them.*

U.S. fighter-bombers, such as these P-47 Thunderbolts, were crucial in driving back German counter-attacks and disrupting enemy movements in Normandy.

Tiger tanks and 88 mm flak guns ripped the British attack force apart. Confusion reigned in the British ranks, and the attack stalled without breaching the German lines. Some 270 burning hulks of British tanks littered the battlefield. While the result was a tactical defeat for the British, it doomed the German defenses in Normandy. Rommel's panzer reserves had to be committed to hold the line for the next crucial two weeks as the Americans gathered their strength to strike, and Caen was now in Allied hands.

At almost the same time, Rommel was hospitalized after his staff car was strafed by British Typhoon fighter-bombers and a group of German officers planted a bomb in Hitler's East Prussian headquarters. The Führer escaped the explosion but emerged from the ruins of his map room even more convinced of the need to stop his generals retreating any more. Von Rundstedt had already resigned and his successor as Commander-in-Chief West, Field Marshal Günther von Kluge, now had even less freedom of maneuver. The defense of Normandy was being directed personally by the Führer.

The *bocage* battle

Holding the German line opposite Bradley was Waffen-SS General Paul Hausser, who had been drafted to lead the German Seventh Army after its commander, Colonel-General Friedrich Dollman, died of a heart attack at the end of June. Hausser was no unthinking Nazi, but a cunning and determined commander with a reputation for being able to improvise skillfully in times of crisis. On the Eastern Front he had commanded the elite II SS Panzer Corps during the battles of Kharkov and Kursk in 1943, at times ignoring Hitler's questionable "fight to the last man and bullet" orders when he thought they threatened his troops with annihilation by Soviet encirclements.

Although he lacked the tank resources of Panzer Group West, later renamed Fifth Panzer Army, under Heinrich Eberbach, which was facing the British and Canadian armies, Hausser deployed his slender forces with great skill to maximize their capability to delay and confound the Americans. His troops turned every village and hedgerow into a fortress, defended by machine guns, mortars, and antitank rockets.

The *bocage* terrain, with its impenetrable networks of sunken roads, thick hedges, dense woods, and picturesque villages, was a nightmare to attack. American tanks and infantry could not maneuver around the German defenses, but had to take each German strongpoint in a slow set-piece attack. Often before the Americans had consolidated their success, they were driven back by a snap German counterattack and had to begin the process all over again.

The first phases of Bradley's campaign in France were conducted in a methodical fashion that reflected his approach to battle. In the days after D-Day, the U.S. Army had concentrated on joining up its two bridgeheads by capturing Carentan at the base of the Cotentin Peninsula on June 12. Over the next two weeks Bradley concentrated on taking the port of Cherbourg, but by the time U.S. troops had reached the city the key shipyards had been systematically demolished by the German defenders and put out of action.

A slow, bloody advance

While Bradley's troops were pushing north to Cherbourg, Rommel had a free hand to reinforce his defenses opposite the American sector, pushing II Parachute Corps and LXXXIV Corps into the line opposite Bradley's men. The attack on Cherbourg exhausted the

A German Panzer IV tank of the Hitlerjugend *SS Panzer Division with its crew. The female names seen in white were written by the young crew, and were probably the names of sweethearts back home in Germany.*

troops taking part, so the newly arrived VIII Corps under Troy Middleton was pushed into the line to help bolster the attempt to achieve a breakout to the south. The experience was very traumatic for the "green" GIs pushed into action for the first time during Bradley's new offensive.

> "This victory cost Bradley another 6,000 casualties, bringing his losses over the past 17 days to 40,000 men killed or wounded"

VIII Corps attacked southward on July 3 against the German LXXXIV Corps and immediately found itself bogged down in heavy fighting. The rate of advance was measured in yards and a high price was paid in blood. The 79th Infantry Division lost 2,000 men in five days and Middleton's other divisions fared little better. In 12 days of fighting VIII Corps's casualties had risen to 10,000. Bradley threw VII Corps into the meat grinder on July 4. It attacked across rain-sodden ground and lost 1,400 men on the first day and 750 on the following day. Eleven days later, the corps had barely moved the front line more than 3 miles (5 km) south, though it had accrued 8,000 casualties doing so.

On July 7 it was the turn of XIX Corps to advance, and Bradley assigned a tank division to it in the hope that it would open a way forward. The result was little better after the tanks became jammed in the narrow, hedge-lined roads and could not maneuver around the German strongpoints. In five days XIX Corps only managed to advance 6 miles (9.6 km).

The only bright point for Bradley in this dismal period was the defeat of a counterattack by the German Panzer *Lehr* Division on July 11, which was driven back with heavy losses.

Bradley was a methodical and determined man who picked himself up from these setbacks, and a new plan was crafted to seize the town of St-Lô and defeat the German II Parachute Corps. After a massed artillery barrage, XIX and V Corps surged forward on July 12 in a pincer attack. In a six-day battle, Bradley fed three divisions into the contest against the battered remnants of the German 3rd Parachute and 352nd Infantry Divisions. The weight of firepower overwhelmed the German defenses, and on July 18 American GIs entered St-Lô to find the town totally devastated. This victory cost Bradley another 6,000 casualties, bringing his losses over the past 17 days to 40,000 men killed or wounded. His front had advanced less than 7 miles (11 km). Many of Bradley's divisions were shattered by this bloody experience, with the long-suffering 90th Infantry Division recording 150 percent casualties among its frontline officers and 100 percent losses in its combat riflemen during the first six weeks of the Normandy campaign.

The one ray of sunshine was the fact that Hausser's battered divisions were in even worse shape than Bradley's troops. Unlike the American First Army, the German forces in Normandy had not received any significant reinforcements during July. Hitler's continued belief that another Allied landing was to be made in the Pas de Calais ensured that the Fifteenth Army, the last uncommitted German force in the West, was kept back from the Normandy Front. A massive Soviet breakthrough on the Eastern Front—Operation Bagration—meant the German armies had to fight on with the resources they had at hand. The divisions manning the Normandy Front boasted little more than a couple of thousand frontline troops to hold their positions. Ammunition and fuel were in short supply because of incessant

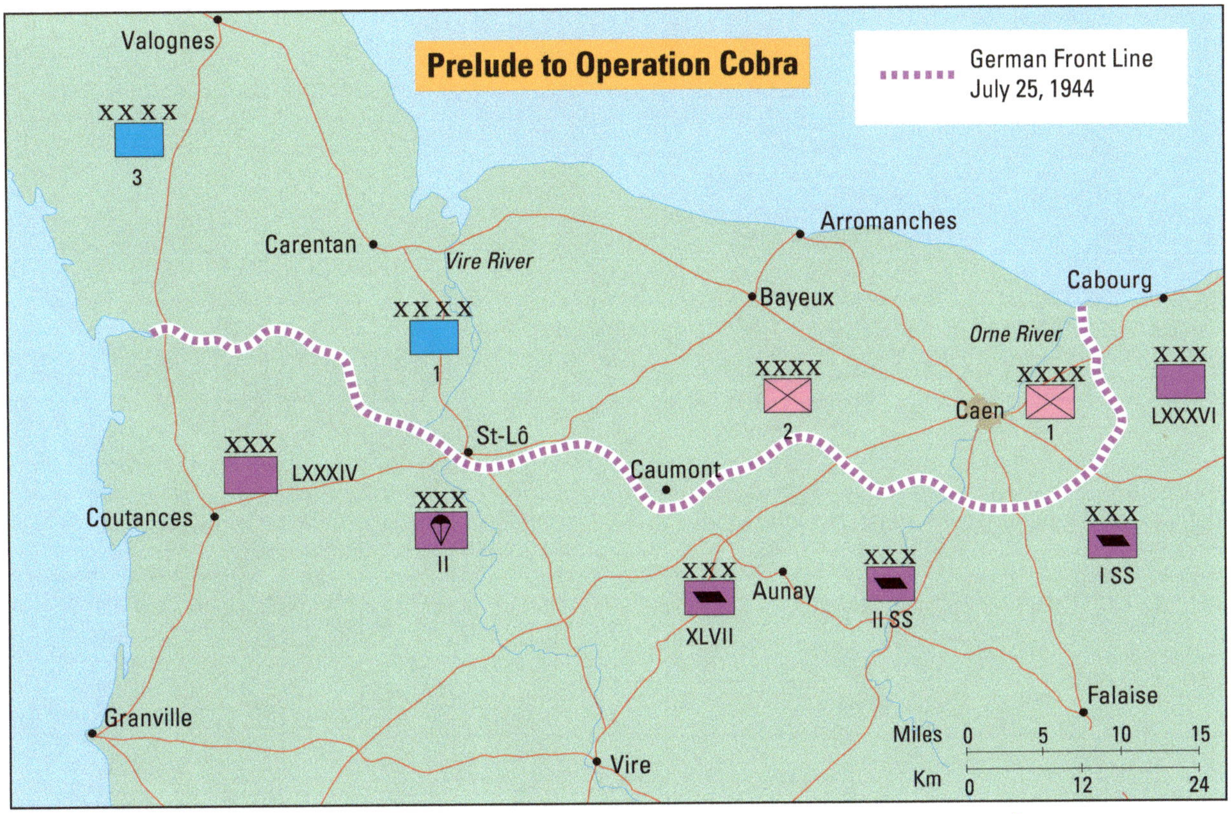

The disposition of German and Allied forces on the eve of Operation Cobra.

Allied bombing of German lines of communication (even food had to be transported to frontline troops at night due to Allied air superiority). Hope certainly seemed to be in short supply among the Germans in Normandy.

Operation Cobra

Morale among Bradley's divisions was clearly shaken by its bruising battles. Something drastic needed to be done to break through the German lines. Even before his attacks were running out of steam around St-Lô, Bradley was planning a major push to achieve a decisive breakthrough. This was dubbed Operation Cobra. It was more than just another thrust through the *bocage*. The firepower of 2,500 heavy bombers and fighter aircraft was to be concentrated on a narrow section of front, and then six divisions, including two armored units, were to roll over the debris of the German defenses. The objective was the town of Avranches at the gateway to Brittany. After Bradley's tanks had reached this objective, Patton's Third Army would be fed into the battle to swing westward and seize the vital Brittany ports. At the same time, Lieutenant-General Courtney Hodges would take over command of the First Army and swing eastward in order to roll toward the Seine River and complete the defeat of the German forces in Normandy. At this stage, a deliberate breakthrough and methodical advance was envisaged, not a dramatic breakout. Only as the battle developed would senior Allied commanders see the potential to encircle and trap the German armies facing them if they acted decisively.

To oversee this vastly expanded American effort, Bradley would be elevated to command the Twelfth

Hitler (center) shows Mussolini (left) the aftermath of the July 20 Bomb Plot. Following this, his acute paranoia led him to distrust his generals even more.

Army Group, in theory putting him on a par with Montgomery himself. Eisenhower, however, would not have his headquarters fully established on the continent until late August, leaving Montgomery effectively in charge of the high-level conduct of the final stages of the Normandy campaign.

Bombers find their target

Bradley briefed his commanders on July 12, and over the next 12 days the preparations for Cobra were put in place. A 6-square-mile (15.5 sq km) section of the front to the west of St-Lô, along the road to Périers, was selected as the bombing target, and July 24 was set as the start date. The key frontline defenses would be saturated by some 5,000 long tons (5,080 tonnes) of high explosives, napalm, and white phosphorus. The Allied air commanders were worried about the danger of hitting their own troops and they proposed a 9,000-foot (2,745-m) safety margin, but Bradley insisted on half this distance. To ease the margin of safety, high-flying heavy bombers would hit the southern fringe of the target box, leaving low-flying fighter-bombers to strike at targets nearer the American lines.

When Allied commanders found out about the July 20 Bomb Plot against Hitler, they realized the urgency of launching Operation Cobra. For George Patton kicking his heels in his command post far behind the front, the tension was clearly too much and he charged into Bradley's command tent, demanding: "For God's sake Brad, you've got to get me into this fight before the war is over."

The first wave of bombers took off on the morning of July 24, but soon the target was obscured by cloud cover, leading to the raid being canceled. Some 500 aircraft did not receive the recall message and dropped 700 bombs on the target area. Unfortunately many landed behind U.S. lines, killing 25 and wounding 130 GIs. The raid alerted the Germans to the fact that a major attack was brewing and their retaliatory artillery bombardment of U.S. staging areas caused heavy casualties and confusion among the assault units.

The following morning the Allied air forces returned in strength to do the job properly. More than 1,500 B-17 and B-24 heavy bombers, supported by an additional 380 medium bombers and 550 fighter-bombers, dropped 4,150 tons (4,215 tonnes) of bombs on the target box. The sheer weight of bombs threw up a huge cloud of debris that obscured the target and led the final wave of aircraft to miss their targets. More than 100 American soldiers were killed and 490 wounded in this attack.

However, the effect on the Germans was devastating, with over 1,000 killed by the bombing alone. In the target zone itself, three battalion command posts were demolished and a regiment was wiped out. The brunt of the bombardment fell on the remnants of the Panzer *Lehr* Division. Its commander, the veteran Fritz Bayerlein, estimated that 70 percent of the troops in the target area were either killed, wounded, stunned, or driven mad. As the surviving Germans emerged from their ruined command posts or bunkers, they were strafed by USAAF Thunderbolts and Mustangs, further adding to the confusion and panic among the demoralized defenders.

Moving up behind a hedge in the* bocage*, three U.S. troops fire on the enemy. The soldier on the far left is firing a fragmentation grenade from his rifle.

Waffen-SS General Paul Hausser. He was a cunning and sophisticated commander, but was ultimately unable to stem the tide of U.S. armor.

The bombing of the American front lines had thrown the assault troops into some confusion, and it took time to get the first GIs to advance into the moonscape caused by the bombing. A handful of German machine-gun nests survived and slowed the American advance to a snail's pace. Bradley and his commanders were momentarily afraid the attack had failed. On the other side of the front, the Germans were also in crisis. Their lines were only holding together by a slender thread. There were no reserves left after Hausser sent his last two battalions to bolster the threatened sector. They proved of little use after U.S. fighter-bombers strafed them as they moved in daylight and decimated their column.

General Günther von Kluge. He later became a field marshal, and took his own life after fearing Hitler suspected him of treason.

The VII Corps commander, Major-General J. Lawton Collins, was made of sterner stuff and decided that he had to commit his two armored divisions to crush German resistance once and for all. His lead tanks had been fitted with improvised hedge plows, called Rhinos, that allowed them to smash through the *bocage* terrain and restore their freedom of maneuver. On the second day of the attack, "Lightning Joe" Collins's troops had all but rolled over the German defenses. The Panzer *Lehr* Division was as good as annihilated and some 600 American tanks were heading south unopposed. On July 28, Hausser threw his final card into the battle, pulling the 2nd SS *Das Reich* Panzer Division and 17th SS *Götz von Berlichingen* Panzergrenadier Division out of the front against VIII Corps and sending them in to hit Collins's columns in the flank. The result was a disaster, with the German panzer columns devastated by Allied airpower as they maneuvered to intercept the Americans. A brief tank battle ensued that temporarily halted VII Corps, but the movement of the two Waffen-SS divisions completely unhinged the German defenses in western Normandy.

VIII Corps strikes

Troy Middleton's VIII Corps had arrived in Normandy a month before as the advance guard of Patton's Third Army, only to find itself attached to Bradley's First Army for the vicious battles in

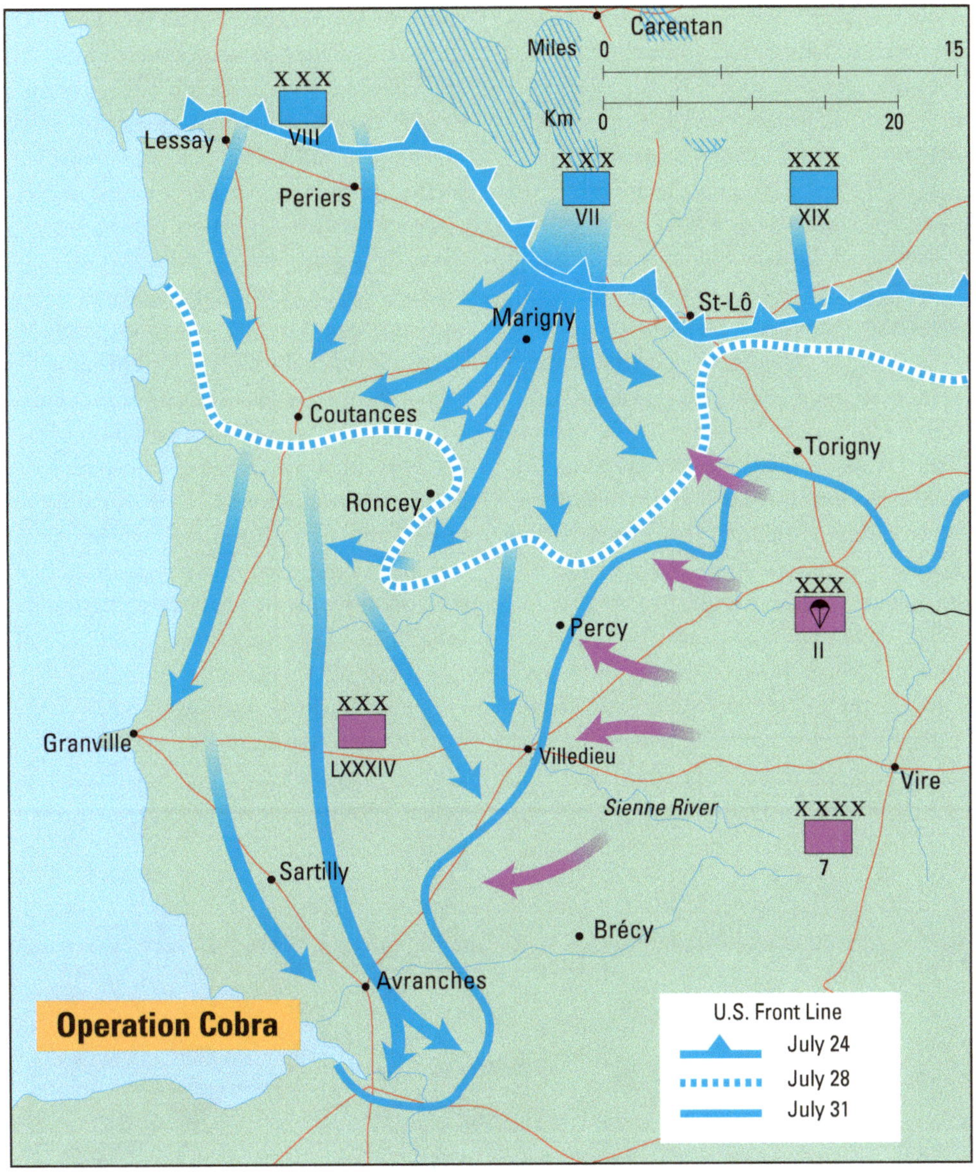

The progression of Operation Cobra as it advanced toward Avranches in July 1944.

the *bocage*. His infantry divisions had certainly been blooded in those deadly duels with Hausser's Seventh Army, but he had yet to commit his armor.

Once Hausser moved his panzers eastward to counter the American breakthrough, Middleton launched the 4th and 6th Armored Divisions forward. The weakened German line broke under the combined weight of some 300 Shermans rolling forward, and the remnants of three German infantry divisions were cut to pieces. The road south was open. On July 28 the "Super Sixth" advanced south through Lessay and headed down the main road to Coutances. Three miles (5 km) to the east, the 4th Armored moved through Périers and also had Coutances in its sights. All that blocked their way was the debris of German columns that had been shot to pieces on the roads by Allied fighter-bombers. By the evening they were through

Coutances and heading south toward Avranches. Combat Command B of the 4th Armored took Coutances in a flanking attack. In the wake of the American tanks came the 79th and 8th Infantry Divisions, which were following close on the heels of the 6th and 4th Armored Divisions, respectively.

> **"Hausser himself had to dodge past an American tank to get back to his headquarters."**

On July 28, General Patton was summoned to Bradley's headquarters to be told that in three days' time the Third Army would be activated and unleashed into Brittany. In the meantime, he would be given interim command of Middleton's troops so he could secure his jumping-off points around Avranches. Without hesitating, Patton drove down to Middleton's headquarters and put the latter in the picture about his intentions.

Early the next morning, Patton headed south to Coutances to get a feel for the battle and encourage his armored spearheads forward. Quickly the troops of VIII Corps got to know what it meant to be under Patton's command. He found the 6th Armored halted at a river while their officers studied a map. Ignoring a group of German troops nearby, Patton strode into the river to test its depth. Finding it was not at all deep, Patton unleashed a torrent of expletives to get his tank crews moving. Patton's next target was a battalion of the 90th Infantry Division whose men he found digging foxholes. "It is stupid to be afraid of a beaten enemy," he shouted at the cowering troops. Suitably invigorated with fighting spirit, Patton's spearheads spent July 29 motoring at full speed toward the town of Avranches.

The 6th Armored saw action for the first time that day, when Combat

U.S. troops with a destroyed enemy artillery piece after it was attacked by aircraft from XIX Tactical Air Command near Marigny.

Command A, supported by its divisional artillery, forced a crossing of the Sienne River west of Coutances, by fording the shallow stream and scaling the bluffs beyond at twilight after clearing moderate resistance on the north bank. 6th Armored advanced 26 miles (42 km) on its first day in combat. The divisional plan stipulated a development in two columns, with Combat Command A following Combat Command B across the river and then advancing on the left flank. During the following 48-hour period the division swept along the Atlantic coast. The city of Granville was not defended, but Bréhal was surrounded by many strongpoints. More than 800 prisoners were captured during the division's advance.

Eyewitness Report:

"July 29th: Raining—moved out at 0728 hours. Went down St-Lô-Périers highway through Périers. All towns and villages in shambles. Périers almost flattened—people streaming back to their former homes if they can find them. Bivouacked about 6 miles (9.6 km) outside of St-Sauveur Lendelin. Here we go again, moved into new bivouac area 4 miles (6.5 km) north of Coutances. We are taking nearly 1,000 prisoners a day. We lost a half-track, and the men are missing. General Wood led the attack personally.

July 30th: Battalion is the spearhead of drive south. Traffic is pretty heavy. We moved out at 0825 hours traveling south through Coutances; most of city is destroyed. We bivouacked about 3 miles (4.8 km) north of Cérences. Ate then moved out and bivouacked again. Jerries shelled our position, moved out. Used T5 (half-track) to rout out some Jerries, who wouldn't come out. I got one with my machine gun. He was trying to circle us. Moved back in old position. Bivouacked 4 miles (6.5 km) up road. Infantry flushing out hedgerows on either side of us. Haven't had a chance to shave for three days. Got five hours' sleep finally—still eating K rations."

***Corporal Albert O. Maranda,* who served in the 4th Armored Division's 94th Armored Field Artillery Battalion**

Prisoners on their own

The German front was collapsing all around Hausser. He himself had to dodge past an American tank to get back to his headquarters. However, that too was soon surrounded by U.S. troops. To the west the remnants of the German LXXXIV Corps, including the two Waffen-SS panzer divisions, were trapped between VIII and VII Corps at Roucy. Hausser made his own escape during the night and ordered his trapped troops to break out to the west. They managed to fight their way past the American columns in the darkness, but left 4,000 prisoners and hundreds of burnt-out vehicles behind them. In front of Patton's spearhead was nothing but confused and defeated German units fleeing for their lives. XIX Tactical Air Command's fighter-bombers roamed ahead of the American columns strafing any German traffic they could find. The biggest problem for 4th Armored was what to do with all the prisoners it was taking. In the end they were simply disarmed and ordered to march north on their own to find a prisoner-of-war camp. On the evening of July 30, the 4th Armored's Combat Command B rolled into Avranches and found the town deserted of Germans. However, it was soon attacked from the north by a column of several hundred German troops who had been bypassed in the retreat. After a brief firefight the Germans surrendered, but when another group of Germans attacked, the prisoners escaped from the tank company guarding the northern approaches to the town.

A large group of Germans managed to escape westward through Avranches during the night, but with daylight U.S. fighter-bombers appeared and ensured the 4th Armored remained firmly in control of the town.

Rounding up prisoners

A series of mop-up attacks rounded up hundreds of Germans scattered around Avranches. On July 31, fighter-bomber pilots returning from patrol reported that the key bridge over the Sélune River at Pontaubault was undefended, and thus John Wood ordered an immediate attack to seize this golden opportunity.

The Germans, realizing the danger to their position in Brittany, had dispatched a battalion, backed up by assault guns, to secure the bridge before the Americans could get to it. Wood's men were quicker. After his Shermans rolled over the bridge they turned southeast to confront the approaching German column. After a brisk exchange of fire, the outgunned Germans beat a hasty retreat to St-Malo. During the day the 4th and 6th Armored Divisions captured 4,000 prisoners between them and the backup infantry bagged another 3,000 Germans. This was a significant part of the 20,000 captured during the six days of Operation Cobra. In four days of breakneck advance, VIII Corps's total casualties amounted to only 700 killed and wounded. It was a far cry from the *bocage* fighting.

Advance to glory

That evening Patton gathered his staff in the "Lucky Forward" command post to announce that they would assume full operational control of VIII Corps tomorrow, ready for the advance into Brittany. The role of the Third Army would, however, remain secret from the world to maintain the fiction that

U.S. troops enter the French town of Coutances. The 4th Armored Division's Combat Command B had taken the town on July 29.

U.S. tanks and infantry in jeeps advance down a road near Coutances. Most of the buildings have been destroyed by artillery fire.

Patton was still waiting in southeast England to lead the invasion of the Pas de Calais and thus distract the German Fifteenth Army from the Normandy Front. He was in a feisty mood, and concluded his speech this way:

"There's another thing I want you to remember. Forget this ... business of worrying about our flanks, but not to the extent we don't do anything else. Some ... fool once said that flanks must be secured and since then [commanders] all over the world have been going crazy guarding their flanks. We don't want any of that in the Third Army. Flanks are something for the enemy to worry about, not us. I don't want to get any messages saying that 'We are holding our positions.' We're not holding anything! Let the [Germans] do that. We are advancing constantly and we're not interested in holding onto anything except the enemy.... We have one motto: *L'audace, l'audace, toujours l'audace!* [Daring, daring, always daring!] Remember that gentlemen."

CHAPTER 4
HARD-FOUGHT LESSONS

Although the Allies were eventually successful in Normandy, the campaign as a whole revealed a number of shortcomings in Allied planning, not least the failure to prepare soldiers to fight a close-quarter battle in the confines of the *bocage* country. Fighting in such terrain came as a nasty surprise to the U.S. First Army, and it suffered heavy casualties as it tried to destroy the skilled German defense of the hedgerows.

The beginning of Operation Cobra, July 25, 1944: the moment when the Normandy campaign changed from an infantrymen's fight to an armored charge across a 4.5-mile (8-km) front into the heart of France.

Previous pages: ***As enemy defenses buckled, units of the 4th Armored Division reached Coutances on July 30, only to find that the Germans had already left.***

The fight in Normandy's *bocage* country illustrated the problems American commanders had experienced since the U.S. Army first entered combat in North Africa in 1943. While General Bradley and others had counted upon the overwhelming superiority and numerical advantage of American arms, fighting the Germans in the hedgerows demonstrated that war was still the domain of the infantryman and his supporting arms.

German defenses

The elaborate German defenses in the hedgerows presented American infantry and combined-arms commanders with problems that often negated the "school solution" of overwhelming the enemy with fire and maneuver, with little consideration given to the need for a unified combined-arms doctrine.

Indeed, as the German defenders in the hedgerows reminded the attacking American soldiers time and again, it was the defender and not attacker that decided when, where, and how the battle would proceed. By selecting the hedgerow country of Normandy to make its first stand against the U.S. First Army, the Wehrmacht briefly immobilized the overwhelming U.S. advantage in tanks, vehicles, and other mechanized assets and forced the U.S. Army to fight on its terms and over terrain of its choosing.

The result was that the Americans had to fight for nearly every hedgerow, which the Germans had transformed into a mini-fortress. The hedges had to be dealt with by set-piece assault teams in a laborious and time-consuming process that delayed General Bradley's desire to avoid the attrition-style of warfare of World War I.

The figures to the right show that Field Marshal Montgomery's later statement that the battle of Normandy "was fought exactly as planned before the invasion" is incorrect. No planner prior to the landings could have foreseen the difficulties faced by American troops in the *bocage* country, and if they did then the troops were needlessly thrown into the battle unprepared for the ordeal of combat ahead. General Bradley was more correct in his summation that the only alternative for the Allies (British and American forces) was to "smash through" the German frontline defenses, since only a "breakout" would effect a rupture of the enemy lines to enable the American and British forces to utilize their advantages in mobility in a war of maneuver.

While the debate between Montgomery and Bradley continued in the battle of the postwar memoirs as to whose methods were instrumental in the defeat of the German Army during the battle for Normandy, the fact remained that the fighting in the *bocage* country once again brought to the fore the importance of combined arms and the requirements of modern mechanized warfare. This was a fact that had become apparent once in the *bocage*, as it showed that American commanders had neglected to prepare their forces

AMERICAN WEEKLY LOSSES IN THE *BOCAGE*

The savagery of the fighting in the *bocage* can be seen in the American casualties incurred in three weeks of fighting. According to Field Marshal Montgomery, the American casualty figures were quite staggering, and reflected the nature of the fighting in the "bloody *bocage*" of Normandy:

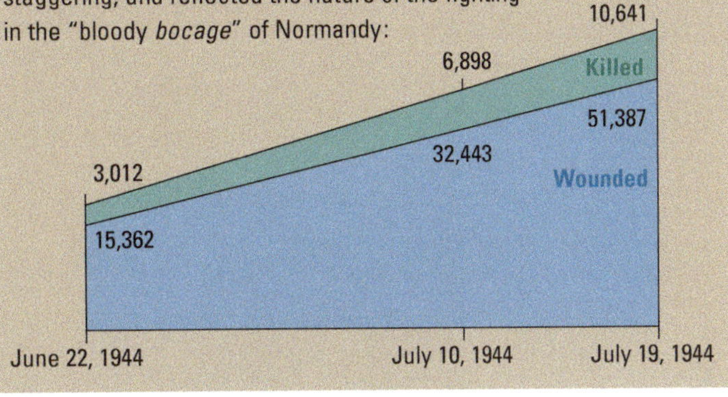

To the east of the U.S. First Army, the British VIII and XXX Corps south of Bayeux began their own push south in Operation Bluecoat.

With the roads out of St-Lô now free of Germans, the armored columns of VII Corps began heading for the next major road junction, at the town of Coutances.

adequately for combat in northwest Europe. While the prewar U.S. Army field regulations made specific mention of the need to train troops in combined-arms warfare, the fact remained that the lessons of the débâcle at Kasserine Pass in February 1943 had not been completely absorbed by American field commanders, specifically General Bradley himself, as the GIs prepared for Overlord.

In fact, General Bradley made little mention or reference to the lessons of Kasserine Pass as applied to preparing the U.S. Army for its grim ordeal in northwest Europe. Indeed, what occurred in the *bocage* country only reinforced the fact that combined-arms training had been seriously neglected in preparing the U.S. Army for combat in France. This proved to be decisive for both the way the campaign was fought in the hedgerows and throughout the remainder of the campaign in France and into Germany.

The need for more effective tank-infantry teams was among the most vital lessons learned in the *bocage* fighting, particularly as U.S. forces began to approach the Siegfried Line. While U.S. commanders became absorbed in the planning and execution of the breakout from Normandy and the rapid movement across France, there was agreement in the after-action reports that the experience gained in Normandy demonstrated the need for closer cooperation between the different combat arms.

In a tactical sense, the First Army proved initially ineffective in its first major battle with the main elements of the Wehrmacht during the fighting in the hedgerows. The elaborate German defenses in the Normandy farmland demonstrated that it was the rifleman, with supporting arms backed up by an excellent logistical and support system behind him, that won battles, and not grand strategy. In the *bocage* fighting, the common denominator between the Americans and Germans was the emphasis the fighting placed on individual combat skills, with advances measured hedgerow by hedgerow and not by large sweeps made or arrows drawn on a map board in a command post or combat operations center.

As for the Germans, only their adoption of elaborate defensive tactics in the hedgerows had averted what they later admitted could have been a total disintegration of their defenses in Normandy. Only by constantly shifting its forces over terrain that channeled the U.S. First Army's broad-front strategy did the Wehrmacht avoid total defeat. Nonetheless, the fact remained that the inability to bring sufficient forces to bear greatly hindered the Germans from capitalizing on their success by concentrating their forces against the various American armies in the *bocage*. Had the Germans been able to concentrate any one portion of their forces against any one of the American divisions in the area outside of St-Lô, they just might have turned the course of battle in any one sector. However, they were forced to contain local thrusts in order to relieve pressure on their own frontline units.

Lack of spirit

One other factor contributed to the German defeat in the battle of the *bocage*, and that was the lack of aggressiveness displayed by some units in making wholehearted offensive efforts. There was solid evidence for this, at least in the views held by Rommel and the other senior German officers concerning the

General Patton took command of VIII Corps and on July 30 launched a drive south, taking Avranches—and these prisoners—on the same day.

results of Panzer *Lehr*'s attack of July 11, 1944. This was noted in the U.S. Army's official history, which stated that there was some dissatisfaction at the high command echelons with overall panzer effectiveness. Fighting spirit was the vital prerequisite for success, and there were signs that it was eroding at troop level.

Part of the "lack of spirit" can be attributed to the shortages the Germans experienced in both men and matériel. Although German troop morale was good, courage alone could not compensate for matériel disadvantages. In short, the Germans could not meet the Allied rate of fire because their transportation system had been bombed incessantly by Allied aircraft night and day, as well as being the target for raids by the French resistance.

Heavy losses

Costly in men and matériel as hedgerow fighting was for the Allies, it was equally expensive for the Germans, who simply could not replace or replenish their forces in a way the First Army could. In an official report issued from OB West in the autumn of 1944, the German high command reported that it had lost 150 Mk IV tanks, 85 Mk V Panthers, 15 Tiger Is, 167 75 mm assault guns (Mk IIIs and Mk IVs), and almost 30 88 mm dual-purpose guns between June 6 and July 9—more than enough to equip an entire Waffen-SS division.

The price in manpower for the Germans was even more staggering. Between June 6 and July 11, at the start of General Bradley's drive toward St-Lô, OB West lost some 2,000 officers and 85,000 enlisted men. In the St-Lô-Cotentin sector, the 243rd Division alone lost over 8,000 men, while the 352nd lost 8,000 officers and men. Panzer *Lehr* lost some 3,140 officers and enlisted men. By July 17, total German casualties had risen to about 100,000, of which 2,360 were officers. Despite Field Marshal von Kluge's desperate attempts at reinforcing the depleted units in Normandy, he sometimes wondered whether or not OKW (the German Supreme Command) appreciated the tremendous consumption of forces on big battle days his divisions were forced to confront during the fighting in the hedgerows.

While the battle in the hedgerows was an infantryman's war, von Kluge and other German commanders, including

First Army M-10s pass through Fontainebleau on the open road to Paris, August 23.

the former commanding officer of OB West, Field Marshal von Rundstedt, correctly saw Germany's only chance of repelling the U.S. First Army was with an active mobile defense. Field Marshal von Kluge wanted "more tanks" to act as the "spine" for the German infantry to deal with any further Allied breakthroughs. Unfortunately, Germany was now scraping the bottom of the barrel in order to stave off defeat in the East and the West. As the fighting in the *bocage* country ended, Field Marshal Montgomery's Twenty-First Army Group and General Bradley's First Army laid the foundation for the Allied victory in northwest Europe, forcing the Germans to concede that the Wehrmacht could never hope to match the Allies in terms of men and equipment, despite its superior tactical and operational abilities.

The Germans, nevertheless, did their best to contain the American breakthrough in Normandy. General Dwight D. Eisenhower acknowledged in his final report of the operations on the Cotentin Peninsula that for six weeks there followed "a grueling struggle to secure a lodgment area of sufficient depth in which to build up a striking force of such magnitude as to enable us to make full use of our potential material superiority. The process took longer than we expected, largely owing to the adverse weather conditions which repeatedly interrupted the flow of men and stores across the Channel. The enemy fought tenaciously to contain our beachheads, though he was at no time able to collect the strength to constitute a serious offensive threat." Tactically and operationally, General Eisenhower admitted that, due to the Wehrmacht's shortage in infantry, its leaders came to depend upon the use of tanks in a defensive role to strengthen its defenses.

GERMAN LOSSES: BATTLE OF NORMANDY

Field Marshal Montgomery in his memoirs provided a rough estimate of German losses during the battle for Normandy:

- Corps and Divisional Commanders Killed or Captured: 20
- Army Commanders Wounded: 2 (Rommel, Hausser)
- Supreme Commanders Dismissed: 2 (von Rundstedt, von Kluge)
- Divisions Eliminated or Mauled: 40

Total Losses (estimate): 300,000
Guns Captured or Destroyed: 3,000
Tanks Destroyed: 1,000

This in turn prevented the Germans from using their qualitative advantage in tanks in more mobile operations, something that Field Marshal von Rundstedt had advocated long before the Allied landings in Normandy. It also prevented the Germans from pulling their armor back to be used once an Allied breakthrough occurred. In one sense, General Eisenhower's comments gave credence to Field Marshal von Rundstedt's earlier conclusions prior to D-Day that a more mobile defense was the best way to defeat the landing, as opposed to Rommel's desire to fight from fixed positions around the beachhead.

As for the fighting in the *bocage* country itself, the view of Lieutenant-General Dietrich von Choltitz perhaps best summarized the fighting for both sides when he commented that the battle in Normandy in the summer of 1944 was "a monstrous bloodbath." For the ordinary American GI, however, who through sheer endurance overcame the German defenses in the hedgerows of Normandy, combat in the *bocage* country brought with it a renewed respect for his German adversary—a respect that remained with him throughout the war.

CHAPTER 5

THE BREAKOUT

In the months after D-Day, the Allies experienced weeks of exhilarating progress alongside periods of agonizing deadlock. During this time, their fortunes alternated between major victories and costly defeats.

Previous pages: ***Smashed German armor litters the countryside around the town of Falaise. The closing of the Falaise Gap was one of the most devastating episodes for the German Army in France, and signaled the beginning of the end of their occupation.***

By the end of July the Americans had broken through the German line, thanks to Operation Cobra, which overwhelmed the worn-out frontline defenses. Hitler ordered six panzer divisions to counterattack and seal the front. After almost two months of continuous fighting, these divisions were little more than weak regimental battle groups. Allied fighter-bombers caught the German tanks in the open and the attack collapsed in chaos. This was the cue for Lieutenant-General George Patton to launch his recently activated Third Army into action, breaking through and racing eastward for the Seine River.

Patton was controversial but talented. He was an expert in fast-moving armored warfare. His Third Army had arrived in France after D-Day, and was fresh. Patton pushed his armored units south and west along the coast. The retreating Germans had no chance to establish a new front line.

Patton's men entered Brittany on July 30. On that same day, Montgomery opened a new attack to the southwest of Caen. Montgomery's new attack was intended to prevent German units from moving westward to deal with Cobra.

Patton's armored units were now moving through Brittany without any real resistance. He asked Allied commanders for permission to turn back to the east, and was ordered to drive behind the Germans toward the Seine River. The German forces on the Normandy Front would have to retreat to avoid becoming surrounded. By August 7, Patton's units had reached the Loire River, some

British troops watch a farmhouse burn in the Normandy village of Christot in June 1944. The Allies had to fight hard to advance through Normandy.

In the days after the D-Day landings, supplies pour ashore from large landing craft to reinforce the Allied bridgehead. Barrage balloons fly overhead to deter German air attacks.

60 miles (96 km) south of their starting point.

The German generals in Normandy argued for a retreat. Hitler instead ordered a counterattack against the town of Mortain. The town stood at the western edge of the fast-developing bulge in the German line. The Germans began Operation Lüttich on August 7. They soon captured Mortain. By the next day, however, the attack was over. The attackers could not overcome U.S. resistance backed by Allied ground-attack aircraft. The Allies could now push ahead with their plan to close the escape routes of the German forces.

The Falaise Pocket

Hitler forbade his troops to even contemplate retreat. Patton's tanks were now closing a huge trap around the German forces that were being driven into a pocket south of Caen. By mid-August the remnants of more than 20 German divisions were pinned into the pocket, with the only escape route being a narrow corridor to the east. On August 20 the pocket was locked shut. Allied aircraft and artillery pounded the pocket for days until resistance ceased. There was no formal surrender or breakout. Individuals made their own choices. The scene Allied troops found as they combed the ruins of the German Army in Normandy was truly apocalyptic. They found 567 tanks, 950 artillery pieces, 7,700 vehicles, and the bodies of 10,000 Germans and the carcasses of tens of thousands of horses. Some 50,000 Germans surrendered, and 20,000 others made their escape on foot through the Allied ring. Of the

SPOTLIGHT

THE LIBERATION OF PARIS

Right: ***Evidence of the often fierce street fighting that took place in the days before the German surrender: a French flag flies over a barricade on a Paris street. There were about 20,000 Resistance fighters in Paris able to take on the Germans, although they were only lightly armed.***

The liberation of Paris represented tangible proof that the Allies were winning the war in western Europe.

Cœur de notre France
Symbole des libertés humaines
L'ECHO D'ALGER

PARIS EST LIBÉRÉ
par les Forces Françaises de l'Intérieur
après quatre ans, trois mois et huit jours d'oppression

MARSEILLE seconde ville de France est délivrée

La France entière et l'Empire ont salué avec une joie délirante la libération de la Ville Lumière
Les Nations alliées se sont associées à l'enthousiasme du peuple français

Ce qu'on verra demain...
Le salut du gouvernement au peuple de Paris
Ce qu'on ne verra plus...
Le général Kœnig annonce la libération de PARIS
LA DÉLIVRANCE DE PARIS fait éclater l'enthousiasme patriotique
DÉLIVRANCE!
UN APPEL du Gouvernement à la population parisienne
Adresse du général d'armée CATROUX gouverneur général de l'Algérie

There was fear on the Allied side that the Germans would fight hard in the French capital, and that such fighting might leave one of the great world capitals in ruins. So the first plans were for bypassing the city and isolating any German garrison.

Hitler had, in fact, decided soon after D-Day that Paris should be razed to the ground rather than fall back into Allied hands: he ordered it should be left a "field of ruins."

As the German armies in northern France were defeated in the Falaise Pocket, there was wrangling about who should be allowed to enter Paris first, and anxiety about what the Germans were planning. In Paris itself, strikes began on August 18, and then Resistance fighters began attacking German troops.

Fortunately, the commander of the garrison of Paris, General Dietrich von Choltitz, refused to carry out Hitler's orders of destruction and set about negotiating a truce with Paris Resistance fighters (this was quite difficult in itself because the resistance was split into various factions, some supporting de Gaulle but many being anti-Gaullist communists). There was street fighting as some Resistance fighters tried to take on the German Army. Although a truce of sorts was called on August 19, violence continued. The Germans burned down the Grand Palais (held by Resistance forces) on August 23.

General de Gaulle was insistent that the capital of France must be liberated by French troops. Eisenhower reluctantly agreed to this, with the proviso that the liberation should involve other Allied detachments also. In the event, the French 2nd Armored Division under General Philippe Leclerc won a race to the capital on August 24 (disobeying orders in order to do so), and de Gaulle himself attended the first of several victory parades in the capital on August 25. Von Choltitz surrendered on the same day.

The relief of the population was almost palpable as French troops moved in. There were painful scenes as collaborators were attacked, but in general the atmosphere was one of joy that the Nazi yoke had been lifted at last.

Above: ***"Paris is freed by the French Forces of the Interior" screams this headline in a newspaper published in French Algeria. The headline simplifies a mass of complex issues. First, the French Forces of the Interior were de Gaulle's wing of the Resistance, and the communists who formed an equally important Resistance organization certainly did not recognize his authority. Secondly, in spite of the fact that there had been fighting in Paris before Allied regular forces arrived, the liberation was achieved by regular forces from outside.***

Right: ***Charles de Gaulle walks down the Champs Elysees in front of the Arc de Triomphe. His belief that French troops should liberate the city led General Leclerc, commanding the French 2nd Armored Division, to disobey orders from his U.S. superior and race into the French capital before any other Allied forces could reach it.***

Left: A Resistance barricade set up on Rue de la Huchette in the 5th Arrondissement. The German garrison had some tanks, and could probably have attacked more of the barricades than it actually did. The Swedish Consul General in Paris, Rauol Nordling, helped establish limits to the fighting that helped the Resistance more than the Germans.

Above: Members of the German administration of Paris surrender to Resistance fighters. On August 16 the Germans executed 35 young Resistance members in the Bois de Boulogne to the west of the city—an act that outraged the public. During the confused fighting of August 17–24 the Germans held many strongpoints, but were not able to clear the streets of Resistance barricades.

38 German divisions committed to the Normandy Front, 25 had ceased to exist. The German Army had lost almost half a million men.

There were now only 70 German tanks and 36 artillery pieces between the Normandy Front and the Rhine. What remained of the German forces in France were in full retreat from the victorious Allied forces. Additional landings in southern France in mid-August completed the rout of Hitler's armies in the West. For a month the pursuit was unrelenting, and by mid-September almost all of France and Belgium had been liberated. Montgomery argued for a narrow advance into Germany, but Eisenhower, the supreme Allied commander, maintained a broad front strategy which gave the Germans some respite. In addition, a fuel crisis forced the Allies to rein in their tank columns to regroup and reorganize before they could begin the final offensive to smash into the heart of Hitler's Reich.

Now the Allies broke out from Normandy and poured toward the western border of Nazi Germany, pursuing a dispirited enemy.

Landings in southern France

Allied morale, on the other hand, was high. It was increased by news that Allied troops had landed in southern France on August 15. Operation Anvil had been planned to take place at the same time as D-Day. It had been delayed, however. There were not enough landing craft for both operations.

Operation Anvil aimed to protect the flank of the Allied armies in northern Europe. It was also planned to open the port of Marseilles as a supply base from the Mediterranean. The landings met with almost instant success. The German troops in the region were generally poor.

By nightfall on August 15, some 95,000 troops had come ashore; only 183 soldiers had been killed.

The Allies forced the Germans to flee north up the valley of the Rhône River. By August 28, they had defeated most of the German troops stationed in southern France. They had suffered relatively few casualties themselves.

On September 11, the southern invasion force linked up with Patton's Third Army outside the city of Dijon. From then on, the Allies could drive toward the German frontier from the Swiss border to the North Sea along an unbroken front. After Falaise, Montgomery's Anglo-Canadian armies started moving along the coast of northwestern France toward northern Belgium.

Paris is liberated

U.S. forces followed a parallel course toward southern Belgium, Luxembourg, and eastern France.

The first big prize of the advance was Paris. On August 19, as the Allies approached, citizens in the French capital rose up against its German garrison. Five days later, the Allies entered the capital amid scenes of great joy. The first troops in the city were the Free French 2nd Armored Division.

The Allied advance stalls

In the excitement, some Allied commanders began to hope that the war might be won before the end of the year. By early September, however, the rush toward the German border was grinding to a halt. Allied troops were tired. Their worn-out vehicles were in urgent need of maintenance. The main problem, however, was keeping the armies supplied.

The Germans had wrecked many ports as they retreated. Other ports, such as Brest in Brittany and Antwerp in Belgium, were still occupied by German forces. The Allies were therefore still being largely supplied from the Normandy beaches. The beaches now lay some 300 miles (480 km) behind the troops. The huge strain on supplying the

Patton (left) talks to British commander Bernard Montgomery (right) and U.S. General Bradley.

GEORGE PATTON (1885–1945)

Patton first made his name during the Allied landings in North Africa in 1942. His career was controversial, however. His thirst for publicity led to clashes with other senior officers. In Sicily in 1943, he slapped two soldiers who had shell shock. Patton was sidelined and only returned to active duty in July 1944. From then until the end of the war, he led the U.S. Third Army in a series of fast-moving offensives. He reacted very quickly to block the German advance in the Ardennes. Patton's troops were also among the first across the Rhine.

At the end of the war, Patton was very outspoken about sensitive political issues. His opinions cost him control of the Third Army. He then took charge of the Fifteenth Army. Patton died from injuries after an automobile accident in 1945.

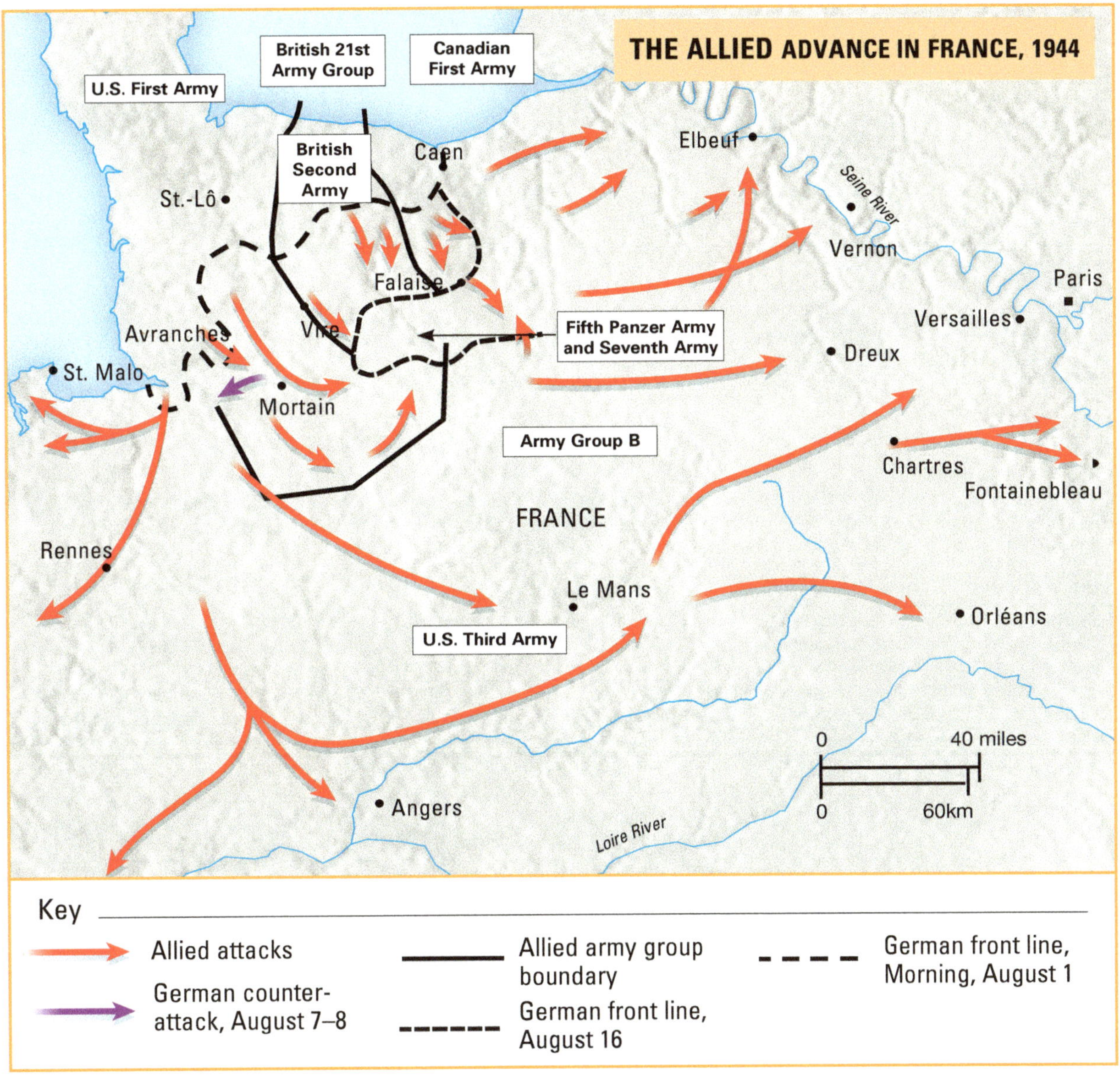

The Allied breakout from the bridgehead in Normandy during the summer of 1944.

armies was unlikely to improve with the onset of winter weather.

In spite of being five years into a long and bloody war, the Wehrmacht had put up an amazing fight in Normandy. While some of the German Army's generals were disaffected with the Führer and were actively plotting to kill him, the rank and file of the fighting troops still believed in Germany's cause. Rommel's infectious enthusiasm rubbed off on the troops being trained to repel the invasion. He was famous for his victories against the British and Americans in North Africa, and many of his troops, along with the divisional officers, were convinced of the logic of Hitler's claim that if the Allied invasion could be thrown back into the sea, then Germany would be able to turn its attention eastward to finish off the Soviets. "When the enemy invades in the West it will be the moment of decision in this war," said Rommel. He was right—but it was the Allies who were victorious.

TIMELINE

SEPTEMBER 1, 1939 – SEPTEMBER 2, 1945

SEPTEMBER 1

POLAND

A German force of 53 divisions, supported by 1,600 aircraft, crosses the German and Slovak borders into Poland in a pincer movement. World War II has begun.

SEPTEMBER 3

BRITAIN AND FRANCE

Britain and France declare war on Nazi Germany after the Nazis ignore their demands to immediately withdraw from Poland.

SEPTEMBER 9

POLAND

A Polish counterattack is launched over the Bzura River against Germany's Eighth Army. It only achieves short-term success. The Polish Army is rapidly falling to pieces under the relentless German attacks.

SEPTEMBER 17–30

POLAND

In accordance with a secret pact with Germany, the Soviet Red Army invades Poland. Little resistance is encountered on Poland's eastern border as the Polish Army is fighting for its life to the west.

SEPTEMBER 18–30

POLAND

Poland is defeated and split into two zones of occupation divided by the Bug River. Germany has lost 10,572 troops and the Soviet Union has 734 men killed in the campaign. Around 50,000 Poles are killed and 750,000 captured.

SEPTEMBER 29

SOVIET UNION

After occupying Poland, the Soviet Union concentrates on extending its control over the Baltic Sea region. During the next few weeks it gains bases and signs "mutual assistance" agreements with Lithuania, Latvia, and Estonia. Finland, however, will not agree to the Soviet Union's demands and prepares to fight.

OCTOBER 14

SEA WAR, NORTH SEA

The British battleship *Royal Oak* is sunk, with 786 lives lost, after *U-47* passes through antisubmarine defenses at Scapa Flow in the Orkneys.

NOVEMBER 30

EASTERN FRONT, FINLAND

A Soviet army of over 600,000 men, backed by air and naval power, attacks Finland. Highly-motivated Finnish troops use their familiarity with the terrain and use their ability to ski through snow-covered areas to launch hit-and-run raids on Red Army units bogged down in the snow.

DECEMBER 16

FINLAND

The Red Army begins a major new offensive. To compensate for their lack of armor and artillery, the Finns use improvised explosive devices ("Molotov Cocktails," named after the Soviet foreign minister) to destroy enemy tanks.

DECEMBER 13

ATLANTIC OCEAN

British ships fight the German pocket battleship *Graf Spee* at Battle of the River Plate. The *Graf Spee* is scuttled by its crew on the 17th.

1940

MARCH 11

FINLAND

The Treaty of Moscow between Finland and the Soviet Union is agreed, ending the Winter War. Finland retains its independence but has to surrender the Karelian Isthmus and Hangö – 10 percent of its territory. Campaign losses: 200,000 Soviet troops and 25,000 Finns.

APRIL 9

NORWAY/DENMARK

A German invasion force, including surface ships, U-boats, and 1,000 aircraft, attacks Denmark and Norway. Denmark is overrun immediately.

APRIL 14–19

NORWAY

An Allied expeditionary force of over 10,000 British, French, and Polish troops lands in Norway.

MAY 7–10

BRITAIN

Prime Minister Neville Chamberlain is severely criticized over the Norwegian campaign. He resigns and is replaced by Winston Churchill.

MAY 10

THE LOW COUNTRIES

German forces invade the Low Countries. But the main German attack will take place in the south, in the Ardennes region of France.

MAY 12–14

FRANCE

German forces reach the Meuse River and fight their way across at Sedan and Dinant on the 13th. German armor advances westward rapidly, opening a 50-mile (75-km) gap in the Allied line. Allied units retreat to the Channel port of Dunkirk.

MAY 26

FRANCE/BELGIUM

Operation Dynamo, the evacuation of Allied forces from the Dunkirk area, begins using small boats and naval vessels.

MAY 31

UNITED STATES

President Franklin D. Roosevelt launches a "billion-dollar defense program" to bolster the armed forces.

JUNE 1–9

NORWAY

After Britain and France reveal to the Norwegians that they are to begin an evacuation, troops begin to withdraw. King Haakon orders his Norwegians to stop fighting on June 9.

June 3–4

FRANCE
Operation Dynamo ends. The remarkable operation has rescued 338,226 men—two-thirds of them British—from the Dunkirk beaches.

June 16–24

FRANCE
Marshal Henri-Philippe Pétain, the new French president, requests an armistice on the 17th. It is signed on the 22nd. Germany occupies two-thirds of France, including the Channel and Atlantic coastlines.

July 1

ATLANTIC OCEAN
The "Happy Time" begins for U-boat crews as their range is increased now that they have bases in French ports. This lasts until October. U-boat crews inflict serious losses on Allied convoys.

July 10

BRITAIN
The Battle of Britain begins. Hermann Göring, the Nazi air force chief, orders attacks on shipping and ports in the English Channel.

July 21

SOVIET UNION
The Soviets annex Lithuania, Latvia, and Estonia.

August 24–25

BRITAIN
The Luftwaffe inflicts serious losses on the Royal Air Force (RAF) during attacks on its main air bases in southeast England, straining the resources of Fighter Command to breaking point in a few days.

August 26–29

GERMANY
The RAF launches a night raid with 81 aircraft on Berlin following a similar raid on London. Hitler is outraged and vows revenge. German aircraft are redirected to make retaliatory raids on London. This relieves the pressure on Fighter Command's air bases.

September 7–30

AIR WAR, BRITAIN
Full-scale bombing raids on London—the "Blitz"—begin with 500 bombers and 600 fighters.

October 28

GREECE
Italy attacks Greece from Albania. The winter weather limits air support and thousands die of cold.

November 5

UNITED STATES
President Franklin D. Roosevelt is elected for a third term.

November 11–12

MEDITERRANEAN
At the Battle of Taranto, British torpedo aircraft from the carrier *Illustrious* destroy three Italian battleships and damage two other vessels during the raid on the Italian base.

December 9–11

EGYPT
The British launch their first offensive in the Western Desert. The Western Desert Force (31,000) attacks the fortified camps that have been established by the Italians in Egypt. Some 34,000 Italians are taken prisoner as they retreat rapidly from Egypt.

1941

January 2

POLITICS, UNITED STATES
President Franklin D. Roosevelt announces a program to produce 200 freighters—"Liberty" ships—to support the Allied Atlantic convoys.

February 14

NORTH AFRICA
To aid the faltering Italians, the first units of General Erwin Rommel's Afrika Korps land at Tripoli.

March 11

UNITED STATES
President Franklin D. Roosevelt signs the Lend-Lease Act that allows Britain to obtain supplies without having to immediately pay for them in cash.

April 6–15

YUGOSLAVIA/GREECE
Thirty-three German divisions, with Italian and Hungarian support, invade Yugoslavia from the north, east, and southeast. German forces also attack Greece from the north.

April 17

YUGOSLAVIA
Yugoslavia surrenders to Germany. Immediately, guerrilla forces emerge to resist the Nazi occupation.

April 27

GREECE
German forces occupy Athens. Campaign dead: Greek 15,700; Italian 13,755; German 1,518; and British 900.

May 20–22

CRETE
A German force of 23,000 men, supported by 600 aircraft, attacks Crete. The Germans launch the first major airborne operation in history.

May 23–27

ATLANTIC OCEAN
British ships find the German battleship *Bismarck* and cruiser *Prinz Eugen* in the Denmark Straits between Iceland and Greenland. The *Bismarck* sinks the cruiser *Hood* and damages the battleship *Prince of Wales*, but is then sunk.

May 28–31

CRETE
Crete falls to the Germans. British losses are 1,742 men, plus 2,011 dead and wounded at sea, while Germany has 3,985 men killed.

June 22

SOVIET UNION
Germany launches Operation Barbarossa, the invasion of the Soviet Union, with three million men divided into three army groups along a 2000-mile (3200-km) front. Army Group North strikes toward the Baltic and Leningrad. Army Group Center aims to take Smolensk and then Moscow. Army Group South advances toward the Ukraine and the Caucasus.

July 31

GERMANY
Reinhard Heydrich, Germany's security chief and head of the SS secret police, receives orders to begin creating a draft plan for the murder of the Jews, which becomes known as the "Final Solution."

September 30

SOVIET UNION
Operation Typhoon, the German attack on Moscow, officially begins.

NOVEMBER 26

PACIFIC OCEAN
The Japanese First Air Fleet leaves the Kurile Islands on a mission to destroy the U.S. Pacific Fleet at Pearl Harbor, Hawaii.

DECEMBER 7

HAWAII
The Japanese attack Pearl Harbor. Over 183 Japanese aircraft destroy six battleships and 188 aircraft, damage or sink 10 other vessels, and kill 2,000 servicemen. The Japanese lose 29 aircraft.

DECEMBER 8

SOVIET UNION
Adolf Hitler reluctantly agrees to suspend the advance on Moscow for the duration of the winter.

DECEMBER 11

AXIS
Germany and Italy declare war on the United States.

1942

JANUARY 10–11

DUTCH EAST INDIES
A Japanese force begins attacking the Dutch East Indies to secure the oil assets of this island chain.

JANUARY 20

GERMANY
At the Wannsee Conference, Berlin, deputy head of the SS Reinhard Heydrich reveals his plans for the "Final Solution" to the so-called "Jewish problem." Heydrich receives permission to begin deporting all Jews in German-controlled areas to Eastern Europe to face either forced labor or extermination.

FEBRUARY 8–14

SINGAPORE
Japanese troops capture Singapore. Japan has fewer than 10,000 casualties in Malaya. British forces have lost 138,000 men.

APRIL 9

PHILIPPINES
Major General Jonathan Wainright, commanding the U.S. and Filipino forces, surrenders to the Japanese.

APRIL 18

JAPAN
Lieutenant Colonel James Doolittle leads 16 B-25 bombers, launched from the carrier *Hornet*, against targets in Japan, including Tokyo.

JUNE 4

PACIFIC OCEAN
The Battle of Midway begins. Japan's Admiral Chuichi Nagumo aims to seize the U.S. base at Midway and then destroy the U.S. Pacific Fleet. Japan deploys 165 vessels, including eight carriers. The U.S. Navy has a smaller force but has three carriers. The loss of half of its carrier strength in the battle, plus 275 aircraft, puts Japan on the defensive in the Pacific.

JUNE 21

LIBYA
Following the Allied withdrawal into Egypt, the Tobruk garrison falls following German land and air attacks.

JUNE 28

SOVIET UNION
Germany launches its summer offensive, Operation Blue, with its Army Group South attacking east from Kursk toward Voronezh.

JULY 4–10

SOVIET UNION
The siege of Sevastopol ends with the Germans capturing 90,000 men.

AUGUST 7–21

GUADALCANAL
The U.S. 1st Marine Division lands on Guadalcanal Island to overwhelm the Japanese garrison.

SEPTEMBER 2

POLAND
The Nazis are "clearing" the Jewish Warsaw Ghetto. Over 50,000 Jews have been killed by poison gas or sent to concentration camps.

OCTOBER 23

EGYPT
The Battle of El Alamein begins. An attack by 195,000 Allied troops against 104,000 Axis men begins.

NOVEMBER 2–24

EGYPT/LIBYA
Rommel, severely lacking supplies, decides to withdraw from El Alamein. Germany and Italy have lost 59,000 men killed, wounded, or captured. The Allies have suffered 13,000 killed, wounded, or missing.

NOVEMBER 19

SOVIET UNION
General Zhukov launches a Soviet counteroffensive at Stalingrad to trap the Germans in a massive pincer movement.

1943

FEBRUARY 2

SOVIET UNION
The siege of Stalingrad ends. Field Marshal Friedrich Paulus and 93,000 German troops surrender.

FEBRUARY 14–22

TUNISIA
In the Battle of Kasserine Pass, Rommel's forces cause panic among U.S. troops. He loses 2,000 men; the Americans 10,000.

APRIL 17

GERMANY
The U.S. Eighth Army Air Force attacks Bremen's aircraft factories from its bases in eastern England. Sixteen of the 115 B-17 Flying Fortress bombers from the raid are lost.

MAY 13

TUNISIA
Axis forces surrender. Some 620,000 casualties and prisoners have been sustained by Germany and Italy. Allied campaign losses: French 20,000; British 19,000; and U.S. 18,500.

JULY 5

SOVIET UNION
Over 6,000 German and Soviet tanks and assault guns take part in the Battle of Kursk.

JULY 9

SICILY
U.S. and British troops begin the attack on Sicily.

JULY 12–13

SOVIET UNION
At Kursk, the Soviets launch a counter-offensive around Prokhorovka and an enormous tank battle develops. The German offensive is defeated.

August 11–17

SICILY
The Germans finally start withdrawing before U.S. forces enter Messina on the 17th.

September 9

ITALY
Lieutenant General Mark Clark's U.S. Fifth Army, plus the British X Corps, lands in the Gulf of Salerno.

September 25

SOVIET UNION
The Soviets recapture Smolensk in their continuing offensive. Germany's Army Group Center is now falling back in some disarray.

November 6

SOVIET UNION
The Soviets recapture Kiev.

December 26

ARCTIC OCEAN
At the Battle of the North Cape, the German battleship *Scharnhorst* is sunk.

1944

January 14–27

SOVIET UNION
The Red Army ends the German blockade of Leningrad. Some 830,000 civilians have died during the siege.

January 22

ITALY
Troops of the Allied VI Corps make an amphibious landing at Anzio, behind the German lines.

March 7–8

BURMA/INDIA
Operation U-Go, the Japanese offensive to drive the Allies back into India by destroying their bases at Imphal and Kohima, begins.

March 20–22

ITALY
Despite further frontal attacks by New Zealand troops, the German defenders repulse all efforts to dislodge them from Monte Cassino.

May 18

ITALY
The Allies capture the monastery of Monte Cassino.

June 6

FRANCE
The Allies launch the greatest amphibious operation in military history—D-Day. Some 50,000 men land on five invasion beaches to establish a toehold in Normandy. Allied casualties are 2,500 dead.

June 19–21

PHILIPPINE SEA
Battle of the Philippine Sea. Japan's Combined Fleet is defeated by the U.S. Fifth Fleet. The Japanese lose 346 aircraft and two carriers. U.S. losses are 30 aircraft and slight damage to a battleship.

June 22

SOVIET UNION
The Red Army launches Operation Bagration against Germany's Army Group Center.

July 20

GERMANY
An attempt is made by German officers to assassinate Adolf Hitler. It fails to kill the Führer.

August 1

POLAND
The Warsaw uprising begins. Some 38,000 soldiers of the Polish Home Army battle with about the same number of German troops.

August 25

FRANCE
The commander of the German garrison of Paris, General Dietrich von Choltitz, surrenders to the Allies.

September 17

HOLLAND
Operation Market Garden, an Allied armored and airborne thrust across Holland to outflank the German defenses, begins. Paratroopers land at Arnhem, Eindhoven, and Nijmegen to capture vital bridges.

September 22–25

HOLLAND
The paratroopers fall back from Arnhem, leaving 2,500 dead behind.

October 2

POLAND
The last Poles in Warsaw surrender as the Germans crush the uprising. Polish deaths number 150,000. The Germans have lost 26,000 men.

October 20

PHILIPPINES
As the U.S. Sixth Army lands on Leyte Island, General Douglas MacArthur wades ashore and keeps a promise he made two years earlier: "I shall return."

October 23–26

PHILIPPINES
Following the U.S. landings on Leyte, the Japanese Combined Fleet is defeated at the Battle of Leyte Gulf.

December 16–22

BELGIUM
Hitler launches Operation Watch on the Rhine, his attempt to capture Antwerp. The thick fog means the Germans achieve complete surprise. But they fail to capture Bastogne.

1945

January 9

PHILIPPINES
The U.S. Sixth Army makes unopposed amphibious landings on Luzon.

January 27

POLAND
The Red Army liberates the Nazi death camp at Auschwitz.

January 28

BELGIUM
The last bits of the German "bulge" in the Ardennes are wiped out. The Germans have had 100,000 killed, wounded, and captured in their defeat. The Americans have had 81,000 killed, wounded, or captured, and the British 1,400 killed.

January 30

GERMANY
The Red Army is only 100 miles (160 km) from Berlin.

February 4–11

SOVIET UNION
Marshal Joseph Stalin, President Franklin D. Roosevelt, and Prime Minister Winston Churchill meet at the Yalta Conference in the Crimea to discuss postwar Europe. The "Big Three" decide that Germany will be divided into four zones, administered

by Britain, France, the United States, and the Soviet Union.

February 13–14

GERMANY
The RAF mounts a night raid on Dresden. The 805 bombers inflict massive damage on the city, killing 50,000 people.

February 17

IWO JIMA
Under the command of Lieutenant General Holland M. Smith, the U.S. Marines land on the island of Iwo Jima. The attackers are hit by intense artillery and small-arms fire from the 21,000-man Japanese garrison.

March 16

IWO JIMA
The island of Iwo Jima is declared secure by the Americans. They have lost 6,821 soldiers and sailors, while of the 21,000-man Japanese garrison, only 1,083 are taken prisoner.

March 22–31

GERMANY
The Allied crossings of the Rhine River begin. German resistance is negligible.

April 1

OKINAWA
Operation Iceberg, the U.S. invasion of the island, commences. The island, only 325 miles (520 km) from Japan, has two airfields on the western side and two partially-protected bays on the east coast—an excellent springboard for the proposed invasion of the Japanese mainland.

April 7

PACIFIC OCEAN
The Japanese *Yamato*, the world's largest battleship, is sunk at sea during an attack by U.S. warplanes.

April 9

ITALY
The final campaign in Italy begins as the U.S. Fifth and British Eighth Armies attack the Germans.

April 12

UNITED STATES
President Franklin D. Roosevelt dies of a cerebral hemorrhage. Vice President Harry S. Truman takes over the position of president.

April 16

GERMANY
The Soviet offensive to capture Berlin commences with a total of 2.5 million men, 41,600 guns and mortars, 6,250 tanks and self-propelled guns, and 7,500 combat aircraft. The Germans have one million men, 10,400 guns and mortars, 1,500 tanks or assault guns, and 3,300 combat aircraft.

April 27

GERMANY
"Fortress Berlin" has been reduced to an east-to-west belt 10 miles (16 km) long by three miles (5 km) wide. German forces within the city are affected by widespread desertions and suicides.

April 28

ITALY
Former Italian dictator Benito Mussolini and his mistress Claretta Petacci are captured by partisans. They are both shot.

April 30

GERMANY
Adolf Hitler and Eva Braun commit suicide in the Führerbunker in Berlin.

May 2

GERMANY
Following a savage three-day battle, in which half the garrison has been killed, Berlin, the capital of Nazi Germany, falls to the Red Army.

May 3

BURMA
Following 38 months of Japanese occupation, Rangoon falls to the Allies without a fight.

June 22

OKINAWA
All Japanese resistance on the island ends. The Japanese have lost 110,000 during the fighting. The U.S. Tenth Army has suffered 7,613 men killed or missing, and 31,807 wounded.

July 17–August 2

GERMANY
The Potsdam Conference takes place in Berlin. The "Big Three"—U.S. President Harry Truman, Soviet leader Marshal Joseph Stalin, and British Prime Minister Clement Attlee (who had defeated Churchill in a general election on July 5)—meet to discuss postwar policy. Japan is informed that an immediate surrender would result in the continued existence of its nation, but further resistance will lead to the "utter devastation of the Japanese homeland." This is a veiled reference to the use of atomic weapons against Japan itself.

August 6

JAPAN
The B-29 Superfortress *Enola Gay* drops an atomic bomb on the Japanese city of Hiroshima, killing 70,000 people and wounding 100,000.

August 9

MANCHURIA
A massive Soviet offensive by 1.5 million men begins against the Japanese Kwantung Army.

August 9

JAPAN
A second U.S. atomic bomb is dropped on Nagasaki. It kills 35,000 people and injures a further 60,000.

August 10

JAPAN
Following a conference, during which the emperor voices his support for an immediate acceptance of the Potsdam Proclamation, Japan announces its willingness to surrender unconditionally.

AUGUST 23

MANCHURIA
The campaign in Manchuria ends in total Soviet victory. The Japanese have had over 80,000 killed and 594,000 taken prisoner. Soviet losses are 8,000 men killed and 22,000 wounded. The Kwantung Army has been destroyed.

September 2

ALLIES
Aboard the battleship *Missouri* in Tokyo Bay, Japanese officials sign the Instrument of Surrender, bringing World War II to a close.

GLOSSARY

amphibious Something that takes place or can operate both on land and in water.

attrition The wearing down of an enemy by actions that use up men or supplies.

battalion A large group of troops with their own headquarters staff.

bivouac A temporary lodging used by soldiers, usually with little or no cover.

bocage A French word describing a landscape in Normandy of small fields separated by tall, thick hedgerows.

breakout A dramatic move in which a military force punches a gap in the defensive line of the enemy.

bridgehead A strong position secured by an attacking force in enemy territory, from which it can then advance.

concentration The gathering of a large amount of troops and military resources in one particular place.

division A small military unit that is capable of taking inedpendent action.

encirclement The act of trying to completely surround an enemy position.

fighter–bomber A warplane that is able to operate both as a fighter and as a close-support bomber to attack targets on the ground.

flank Either side of a military formation.

half-track A military vehicle with wheels in the front for steering but caterpillar tracks in the back for power and grip.

K rations A small package of emergency rations issued to U.S. soldiers.

LCT An abbreviation for Landing Craft, Tank, a vessel that was designed to land tanks on beaches.

logistical Relating to transporting and supplying a military force.

matériel A military word for the supplies required for a campaign, such as weapons, ammunition, and hardware.

mechanized warfare Warfare that is based on vehicles such as tanks, trucks, and airplanes.

morale The fighting spirit of the combatants, and their confidence about achieving victory.

Panzer German word for tank.

pillbox A low-roofed concrete emplacement for defensive weapons such as machine guns or antitank guns.

pocket A military position in which a group of troops is entirely surrounded by the enemy.

reserves A large body of troops that are held back from the fighting in order to provide reinforcements where necessary.

strafe To repeatedly attack a target with machine-gun fire or bombs from low-flying aircraft.

strategy A detailed plan for achieving success.

strongpoint Any defensive position that has been strengthened to withstand an attack.

tactical Relating to the immediate aims of a military action, rather than to the overall goals of a war or campaign.

treason The crime of betraying one's country, government, or military colleagues.

FURTHER READING

BOOKS

Davenport, John. *D-Day and the Liberation of France* (Milestones in Modern World History). Chelsea House Publishers, 2010.

Immell, Myra. *D-Day* (Perspectives on Modern History). Greenhaven Press, 2012.

Miller, Terry. *D-Day: The Allies Strike Back During World War II* (24/7 Goes to War: On the Battlefield). Scholastic Library Publishing, 2009.

Murray,Doug. *D-Day: The Liberation of Europe Begins* (Graphic Battles of World War II). Rosen Central, 2007.

Stein, R. Conrad. *World War II in Europe: From Normandy to Berlin* (The United States at War). Enslow Publishers, Inc, 2011.

Williams, Brian. *The Normandy Beaches* (A Place in History). Arcturus Publishing, 2011.

Zaloga, Steven. *The Most Daring Raid of World War II: D-Day – Pointe du Hoc* (The Most Daring Raids in History). Rosen Publishing Group, 2011.

WEB SITES

Due to the changing nature of Internet links, Rosen Publishing has developed an online list of Web sites related to the subject of this book. This site is updated regularly. Please use this link to access the list:

http://www.rosenlinks.com/WW2/Alli

INDEX

INDEX